STATIONS OF THE LIGHT

STATIONS

of the

LIGHT

• • •

RENEWING THE ANCIENT
CHRISTIAN PRACTICE OF THE
VIA LUCIS AS A SPIRITUAL
TOOL FOR TODAY

• • •

Mary Ford-Grabowsky

IMAGE BOOKS · DOUBLEDAY

NEW YORK   LONDON   TORONTO   SYDNEY   AUCKLAND

To

SISTER MARY JOSE HOBDAY, O.S.F.,

who is

a *via lucis*

AN IMAGE BOOK

PUBLISHED BY DOUBLEDAY
a division of Random House, Inc.

IMAGE, DOUBLEDAY and the portrayal of a deer drinking from
a stream are registered trademarks of Random House, Inc.

Book design by Stephanie Huntwork

Library of Congress Cataloging-in-Publication Data
Ford-Grabowsky, Mary.
Stations of the light : renewing the ancient Christian practice of the via
lucis as a spiritual tool for today / Mary Ford-Grabowsky.—1st ed.
        p. cm.
ISBN 0-385-51165-5 (alk. paper)
1. Jesus Christ—Forty days—Meditations. I. Title.

BT485.F67 2005
232.9'7—dc22   2004056871

PRINTED IN THE UNITED STATES OF AMERICA

March 2005

First Image Books Edition

1   3   5   7   9   10   8   6   4   2

Contents

A c k n o w l e d g m e n t s

To Tom Grady, my deepest possible gratitude and admiration for being an outstanding agent and a source of faith and light in a very dark time of history.

To Trace Murphy, a distinguished editor who is a joy to work with, my most heartfelt thanks.

To Fr. Sabino Palumbieri, for infusing church history with "the joy that is full and more than full," for invaluable helpfulness to me, and for the beauty of spirit and radiant mind he brought to our correspondence: *Thank you!*

To Monsignor Gianfranco Ravasi of the Biblioteca Ambrosiana in Milan, my deepest gratitude for gracious assistance.

To Archbishop Angelo Amato, SDB, of the Congregazione per la Dottrina della Fide in Vatican City, my most sincere gratitude for kind assistance.

To Fr. Richard Alejunas, SDB, Editor of the Salesian Bulletin, New Rochelle, New York, special warm thanks for helping with research.

To the library staffs at Harvard Divinity School, Newton-Andover Theological, and Boston College, for your warm and friendly help with research.

To the pastor and staff of St. Patrick's Parish in Natick, Massachusetts, for setting aside an evening in the Easter season for the congregation to pray the *Via Lucis* (Way of Light). It was a beautiful experience, the church was full, and hopefully other parishes will quickly follow your lead.

To Adam Cardinal Maida, since 1990 Archbishop of the Archdiocese of Detroit, whose inspiring pastoral leadership led to the creation of St. John's Center for Youth and Family, where the first set of Stations of the Light in the U.S. were created, heartfelt gratitude.

To Axel Grabowsky, loving thanks for our lifetime journey together, and for the breadth of research and knowledge you contributed to this book.

To Tara Grabowsky, my daughter, whose healing gifts, deep women's spirituality, and, most of all, love nurtured me through the writing of this book.

To Kevin Potts, my son-in-law, a huge soul, who shared his loving peacefulness with me while I was working on this manuscript.

To Eryk Hanut, who knows the Way of the Cross and the Way of Light more deeply than anyone I know, thank you with all my heart for a flawless friendship and for using your artistic genius in many media to give the world sacred light.

To Lauren Artress, who has taught an entire generation the value of spiritual practice: my deep admiration, respect, and gratitude.

To Dorothy Walters, beloved companion on the way, thank you for all your support, encouragement, and wisdom.

To Paola Biola, for reading parts of the manuscript and giving me invaluable feedback, loving thanks.

To Adriana Diaz, cherished friend, for the extraordinary, uplifting gift of presence at every step of the way: Thank you!

To three of my students at UCS, very special thanks and love:

> S. Malia Dominica Wong, the most spiritually refined person I have ever taught, for teaching me.

> Debbie Sloan, for her inspiring spiritual attainment and contagious capacity for joy.

> Georgiana Lotfy, a creative spiritual leader who "sees the world in all its sacred radiance."

Preface

A few days after Jesus' death, something happened. His closest followers began seeing him again and interacting with him. Over the course of the next seven weeks, from the day we call "Easter" to the day known as "Pentecost," these men and women received some of his most moving and beautiful teachings about the wisdom of God. Then, when they were fully prepared to carry on his work, Jesus went out of their sight. The small community gathered with Mary, his mother, in a place called "the Upper Room," where they had met with their beloved Teacher on many happy occasions in the past, and began to pray.

While praying, the small community was overtaken by a collective experience of ecstasy that words could not adequately describe. It was like hearing a rushing wind and feeling flames set their souls on fire, and it gave them the courage to go into foreign countries, as Jesus had instructed them, to teach, to preach, to heal, and to baptize. At some point they began speaking of "Jesus" as "the risen Lord," the Christ promised in the Scriptures who would be the first person to ever fully keep his people's covenant with God. Before long a "Jesus movement" had begun that spread far and wide the most sublime spirituality of love that the world has ever known.

The Christian story has never ceased captivating me from earliest childhood to the present day. I began reading the Christian mystics at the age of eight and spent some of the happiest hours of my childhood at my aunt's big convent on a hilltop in Brighton, Massachusetts, learning all I could about the people in the sacred story and saturating myself in the beauty of silent prayer. In college I minored in theology (no major was offered in those days) and later spent seven rich years in seminary feasting on the endless dimensions of faith, learning, and love that the Christian story has been inspiring for two thousand years. Pilgrimages to the Holy Land and to Rome were on my must-do list by the time I was ten.

When I finally visited Rome for the first time to see the Sistine Chapel, the *Pietà*, and the other great works of art and architecture that abound in that magnificent city, I had no idea that a trip to the Catacombs would result in a book called *Stations of the Light*, but that is precisely what happened. My husband, our little girl, and I drove slowly along the beautiful Appian Way, which looked like burning amber, to the Catacombs of San Callisto. There, leaving behind the glowing light and warm air of the Via Appia, we found ourselves in a cool and dark, narrow, low-ceilinged corridor that felt eerie, yet like a very sacred space.

We began walking along the corridors, fascinated by casket-sized indentations in the walls where Christians were once buried, when I noticed the outline of a fish, the *ichthys*, one of the earliest symbols for Christ, carved on a wall. There were other drawings and inscriptions on most walls and on many ceilings, some of which, the guide said, were ancient graffiti. One of the inscriptions was a fragment from Saint Paul's letter to the church at Corinth, 1 Corinthians 15:3–8, which today is the basis for the new and very joyful devotion known as the *Via Lucis*, the Way of Light.

The following pages will contain the inscription and explain how the Way of Light and the Stations of the Light came to be. The second part of the book contains spiritual practices drawn from both Eastern and Western religions for expanding our souls, deepening our spiritual sensitivities, and rescuing the world from the violent pathology that is infecting and sickening it. As the Dalai Lama has said, "Spirituality is the immune system of the world." Clearly, much more spiritual practice is needed on all our parts if the world is to be healed.

Part I

• • •

INTRODUCTION

THE WAY OF LIGHT

A New Journey

This book is an invitation to practice a new spiritual journey called the Way of Light, which celebrates fourteen of the most inspiring events in the post-Resurrection life of Christ on earth. These great archetypal moments in the Christian story, which are called the Stations of Light, have been known and cherished since the first century, but as far as we know were never gathered into a precise devotional practice until the present time. Also known as the Via Lucis and Way of Resurrection, this devotion follows the footsteps of the risen Christ and his friends for fifty days, from the dawn of the first Easter Sunday through Pentecost, along a path of transforming joy.

Part I of this book describes the rich origin and significance of the new devotion for Christian spiritual life. Praying the Stations offers gifts of grace that awaken the body, illumine the mind, and train the heart for happiness. Among the gifts are love and faith, which are the purpose of all prayer, as well as peace and comfort, reverence for the sacred, and joyful optimism about the future and growing toward elderhood. Part I also contains a chapter on the Way of the Cross to show how its focus on a single tragic day of Jesus' life is like telling only the first part of a story and leaving out the happy ending. The Way of Light takes up the story with the Resurrection and celebrates the awe-inspiring events that occurred from then on.

Part II, the devotional section of the book, contains spiritual practices for praying the Stations of the Light. The practices for each station are designed and arranged for maximum soul-building, community-building, and loving intimacy with God. They involve the whole person—body, mind, and spirit. One exercise teaches relaxation and centering; others elicit your insights and new ideas; some release imagination and creativity; while others evoke deep feelings and thoughts; still another invites movement to awaken the body (which has been called body-prayer).

Here is the Way of Light:

Station 1: Jesus rises from the dead (Matthew 28:5–6).

Station 2: Women find the empty tomb (Matthew 28:1–6).

Station 3: The risen Lord appears to Mary Magdalene (John 20:16).

Station 4: Mary Magdalene proclaims the Resurrection to the apostles (John 20:18).

Station 5: The risen Lord appears on the road to Emmaus (Luke 24:13–27).

Station 6: The risen Lord is recognized in the breaking of the bread (Luke 24:28–32).

Station 7: The risen Lord appears to the disciples in Jerusalem (Luke 24:36–39).

Station 8: The risen Lord gives the disciples the power to forgive (John 20:22–23a).

Station 9: The risen Lord strengthens the faith of Thomas (John 20:24–29).

Station 10: The risen Lord says to Peter, "Feed my sheep" (John 21:15–17).

Station 11: The risen Lord sends the disciples into the whole world (Matthew 28:16–20).

Station 12: The risen Lord ascends into heaven (Acts 1:9–11).

Station 13: Waiting with Mary in the Upper Room (Acts 1:12–14).

Station 14: The risen Lord sends the Holy Spirit (Acts 2:2–4).

The Empty Tomb: A Lost Symbol

The Way of Light opens at dawn with the dark beauty of an empty tomb. Like a cave where a holy man meditates for years in search of illumination, hewn out of natural rock, this most sacred of all sacred spaces has a natural earthen floor and opens onto a lush garden that is almost invisible in the pale light of dawn, but soon will be radiant. Angels in dazzling white clothing make the astounding announcement that the cave is empty because Jesus, whose body was placed there three days ago, is risen from the dead.

The empty tomb with all its dark, silent fertility is one of the two primary symbols of the Christian faith but has long been neglected in favor of the other, the cross. The two great images should be seen as inseparable complements of one truth, although they are virtually opposites in meaning. The cross is a place of cruelty and violent death, while the empty tomb is a site of new life. On the cross, Jesus is totally emptied out, and it appears that mindless human destructiveness wins a battle over the forces of goodness, but in the empty tomb, God's infinite creative power restores what evil human behavior temporarily took away.

Without the empty tomb and all that it births, from the joy of Easter to the ecstasy of Pentecost, the Christian story would end meaninglessly with Jesus dehumanized on the cross, defeated and discredited. His traumatized followers would flee for their lives in fear of a similar fate and never regroup, with the result that the spiritual community that has endured for two thousand years might never have come to be. Jesus, his mother, Mary Magdalene, Peter, and all the other protagonists in the story would have slipped out of human memory. Without the Resurrection, Jesus' destiny would be no grander than that of other "lower-class dissidents," as the Romans termed young men whom they crucified for disturbing the peace.

But the story does not end there, of course. Only a few days after Jesus' death, he reappears, and that is the whole point of the story. The tomb opens like a womb giving birth, and he is released into Resurrection-life. The rebirth archetype is so incomprehensible and overwhelming that angels are sent to enlighten humankind with the mind-bursting news of life after death. Throughout the subsequent fifty days of the first Easter season, the light grows increasingly brighter. The journey that began in the first light of dawn on Easter Sunday morning progresses through varying degrees of sunlight to its culmination in blazing fiery light on Pentecost. Here, we followers of the Way learn to believe that darkness is always overcome by Light. We need only wait for it.

In the dazzling light of the Pentecostal flames, with Jesus' disciples gathered around his mother, one in prayer and faith and love, united in the new spiritual community that is being born, the Way of Light draws to a close, and the two paths on which Jesus journeyed, the Way of Sorrows and the Way of Light, are brought into their right relationship as two halves of a whole, two complementary phases of a single path.

Why Did the Cross Become Dominant?

Why did Western Christianity allow the cross to become the dominant symbol while the empty tomb signifying the Resurrection lay in the background like an unexplored treasure chest? How is it possible that, in the story of ancient Rome's brutality, the archetypes of negativity could overpower the breathless joy and heart-stopping beauty found on the Way of Light? This difficult question requires painstaking research and reflection that lies outside the scope of this book.

A tradition exists (that will be mentioned in Chapter 2) according to which Mary the mother of Jesus made daily visits to the sacred sites where Jesus suffered and died as well as to the sites of the Resurrection and ascension. If this were historically accurate, it would suggest that early Christianity honored both the sorrowful and joyful mysteries of Jesus' life, not only the ones pertaining to suffering. Nevertheless, the Way of the Cross emerged markedly over the Way of Light and has colored Christian spiritual practice since the Middle Ages.

Alternative Versions of the Way of Light

As the scenes commemorated on the Way of the Cross changed rather dramatically over the centuries (which will be discussed in Chapter 2), different versions of the Stations of the Light are possible. For example, in this book, the Second Station describes the women's discovery of the empty tomb according to Matthew's Gospel, which has similarities to Mark's and Luke's versions of the story. But one could also use the Gospel according to John to focus on the touching story of Peter's running with another disciple to the empty tomb after hearing from Mary Magdalene that Jesus is risen.

In the case of the Emmaus story, it can be presented as a single station or divided into two stations as in this book, to highlight the importance that each part offers for spiritual life today. The Fifth Station, on the road to Emmaus, has too much to say about journeying with the risen Lord to risk underemphasizing it. Similarly, recognizing Christ in the breaking of bread at the Emmaus inn is the essential Eucharistic image of the Way of Light and far too important to minimize.

Also, the Tenth Station can be divided into two parts, one commemorating Christ's cooking breakfast for the disciples at the Sea of Tiberias, and the next focusing on the moving scene where he tells Peter, "Feed my sheep." Then, too, the scriptural material found in Station 3 (the risen Lord's appearance to Mary Magdalene) and Station 4 (his sending her to proclaim the Resurrection) could be condensed into a single station honoring Mary Magdalene.

Similarly, the Thirteenth Station (waiting with Mary the mother of Jesus for Pentecost) could be combined with the Fourteenth Station (Pentecost).

But all of these versions of the Way of Light are faithful to the Gospels, which is the essential criterion for arranging them.

Was the Way of Light an Early Christian Practice?

It is not unreasonable to imagine that early Christian pilgrims who devoutly walked the Way of the Cross may have wanted to pray also at the places where the post-Resurrection events took place in order to bring their painful journey to a conclusion in the joyful events of the Way of Light.

If so, they would have begun the journey in Jerusalem at the site of the tomb where Jesus rose from the dead and in the garden where he appeared to Mary Magdalene (today's Church of the Holy Sepulchre).

They would have then left the old city of Jerusalem on the western side to follow the seven-mile road to Emmaus and stopped at the inn where Jesus broke bread with two of his disciples.

The Upper Room would be the next logical stop, but, as four stations are set there, this one might have been postponed for one all-encompassing visit at the end of the Way of Light. In that case, the pilgrims might have proceeded to the Sea of Tiberias to sit on the shore where the risen Lord cooked breakfast for his beloved friends and gave Peter the great teaching, "Feed my sheep."

After that, they might have gone to Mount Olivet and climbed a short distance up the side of the low mountain to pray at the location of the Ascension, presumably in the very olive groves mentioned in the New Testament.

In all likelihood the journey would have concluded back in Jerusalem, in the Upper Room where Jesus and his disciples gathered on many sacred occasions. Here he appeared in his Resurrection body to a large number of followers, transformed the apostle Thomas's raging doubt to faith, and brought his post-Easter ministry to a magnificent close by sending the Holy Spirit on Pentecost to be with his followers "always."

No evidence has yet been uncovered that proves conclusively such a pilgrimage ever took place, while there is extensive evidence that pilgrims followed the Way of the Cross (as Chapter 2 explains). To what extent early Christians may have walked the Way of Light could be proven only by future discoveries of unknown ancient manuscripts that allude to such a practice. There is always hope of that eventuality, especially in light of the dramatic discoveries of the Gnostic Gospels in 1945 near the town of Nag Hammadi in Upper Egypt and of the Dead Sea Scrolls in 1947 in a cave in Qumran on the shore of the Dead Sea.

Where Has the Way of Light Been?

While the Way of the Cross (Via Crucis) charts the anguished course of Jesus' horrendous last hours and death, the Way of Light (Via Lucis) celebrates the most joyful time in the Christian calendar, the fifty days of the paschal season from Easter to Pentecost. The idea for fashioning the Way of Light was sparked by an ancient inscription found on a wall of the San Callisto Catacombs on the Appian Way in Rome. The enormous cemetery is named for Saint Callistus, the sixteenth pope (217–222), and occupies ninety acres with a honeycomb of corridors twelve miles long extending, on four levels, sixty feet deep.

The Saint Callistus inscription, known as "Paul's Gospel," comes from a letter he wrote to the church at Corinth, 1 Corinthians 15:3–8, in light of reports that some members were denying the Resurrection. Here is what he said:

The Inscription, San Callisto Catacombs

I delivered to you as of first importance what I had been taught myself, namely that Christ died for our sins in accordance with the scriptures, that he was buried, that he was raised to life on the third day, in accordance with the scriptures, and that he appeared to Cephas, then to the twelve. Then he appeared to more than five hundred brothers at one time, most of whom are still alive, though some have died. Then he appeared to James, and then to all the apostles. Last of all, he appeared to me, too, as though I was born when no one expected it. (1 Corinthians 15:3–8)

In contrast to the radical suffering recalled by the Way of the Cross, the Way of Light issues from these comforting, hopeful New Testament verses about the triumphal events in the life of the post-Easter Christ. Anonymous second-century members of the believing community in Rome presumably wrote the words in the Catacombs as a reminder to all who would read them that, for Christians, death ends in resurrection, sorrow in joy, and history in the final triumph of grace.

With this awareness in mind, a spiritual group guided by Fr. (Father) Sabino Palumbieri, a Salesian priest in Rome, conceived a new idea in the 1990s. It was decided to combine the joyful events mentioned in the Saint Callistus inscription with other post-Resurrection events to create a new set of stations. These new stations would emphasize the positive, hopeful aspect of the Christian story without losing awareness of the darkness recalled in the Way of the Cross. Thus the Way of Light, an optimistic complement to the Way of the Cross, was fashioned of fourteen stations commemorating the Easter season and paralleling the fourteen Stations of the Cross.

The new devotion (which as we have said was probably an ancient devotion, though not precisely in this form), was first blessed on Easter Sunday, 1994, in Turin, Italy, at the hill of Becchi, the birthplace of Saint John Bosco (1815–1888), the founder of the Society of St. Francis de Sales (Salesians). On that day, lovely wood carvings of the fourteen Stations of the Light created by the artist Giovanni Dragoni were displayed on the Hill of Becchi; today, they can be seen at the Sanctuary of Our Lady of the Rosary, Pompeii, Italy.

The Via Lucis formally became a Roman Catholic devotion at the end of the twentieth century when the Vatican was preparing the Jubilee Year 2000 campaign and searching for new devotions appropriate to the millennial transition and yet faithful to the Christian tradition. Pope John Paul II declared the year 2000 a year of thanksgiving, expressed through the Eucharist (which comes from the Greek word eukharistia, meaning "thanksgiving").

Long before that, the Second Vatican Council (1962–65) had generated widespread awareness, especially among the laity, of a perplexing negative cast to the church's preaching and teaching through an overemphasis on suffering, evil, sin, and guilt. Vatican II attempted with some success to bring the negative and positive into a better balance, one that painted a more accurate portrait of the real relationship between sorrow and joy in the Gospels and in life.

The Congregation for Divine Worship in Vatican City published the following statement about the Way of Light in the *Directory of Popular Piety and the Liturgy* in December 2001:

> The *Via Lucis* is potentially an excellent pedagogy of the faith since: *per crucem ad lucem* [through the cross to the light]. Using the metaphor of a journey, the *Via Lucis* moves from an experience of suffering, which in God's plan is part of life, to the hope of arriving at man's true end: liberation, joy, and peace which are essentially paschal values.
>
> The *Via Lucis* is a potential stimulus for the restoration of a "culture of life" which is open to the hope and certitude offered by faith, in a society characterized by a "culture of death," despair and nihilism.

Awareness grew that a Via Crucis without a Via Lucis was like a bird with only one wing, utterly incapable of flying. Significant strides have been made in bringing the positive and negative into a right relationship since Vatican II and, hopefully, as the Way of Light spreads around the world, it will contribute significantly to an attitude of Christian joy. We are called to be *crucifers* and *lucifers*, cross-bearers and light-bearers, not literally like the ministers who carry the cross and light at the beginning of every liturgical procession, but symbolically as pilgrims who were given this vocation at baptism.

· PEOPLE ON THE WAY OF LIGHT ·

JESUS OF NAZARETH

Jesus' life was for over thirty years a continual Gloria to God. A more sublime teacher of love and the wisdom of God than the world had ever known, he spent himself in a public ministry for some three years, walking the baked earth roads of ancient Galilee and drawing crowds of worshipers everywhere he went. Jesus healed people of all kinds of infirmities while telling stories of breathtaking beauty, offering forgiveness, and preaching the Kingdom of God as though a new world were soon to come that would overcome injustice with compassion. Some were so moved by him that they gave away all their possessions to the poor and followed him, embracing his itinerant lifestyle of faith and love in the hope of personal salvation and that of all humankind.

Jesus came from Nazareth, a disreputable town with a population estimated between 200 and 2,000 located about a hundred miles north of Jerusalem and a day's walk from four bustling cosmopolitan cities, one featuring a theater. He was born to a poor Jewish family from the lowest class of society that was more marginalized than even the despised peasants who at least owned a parcel of land. But Jesus' Jewish family was deeply devout and undoubtedly schooled him in the Torah at the synagogue in Nazareth, where the Scriptures must have set fire to his young soul. He earned a meager living as a *tekton*, the Greek word for woodworker.

Probably while in his twenties, he decided to be baptized by his cousin John, the leader of a religious reform movement based in repentance. At the time of the baptism, immersed in the Jordan River, Jesus saw the Spirit of God descend over him in the form of a white dove and heard words of infinite tenderness: "This is my beloved son, with whom I am well pleased" (Mark 1:11b). As though his eyes had seen into eternity, he received in this mystical experience a surge of sublime self-understanding and certainty about his divine calling that words alone could not have conveyed.

The magnitude of his calling led to strong temptations to use his power and knowledge for personal gain, but through deep prayer and fasting he dismissed all temptations and kept his people's broken covenant with God, the first person ever to do so perfectly. Sometime in his twenties, Jesus undertook the public ministry that would lead to his harrowing death on a cross.

The Passion of the Christ

Jesus' moving parables and stories, which today nourish the spirit, barely concealed a trenchant criticism of the priestly hierarchy of his time who enforced a hypocritical "purity code" composed of hundreds of stifling laws, rules, and regulations. The "purity code" forbade what was seen as impure, unclean, and unholy. Certain foods (such as pork), certain people (such as tax collectors), and many human behaviors were impure. Only official rituals could purify the unclean, and the religious establishment heavily taxed the poor and additionally exacted unjust fees from them for obligatory purification rites.

Into this "den of thieves" that was so brutally exploiting the poor, Jesus brought a message of love instead of law, and a God of unconditional love instead of the cruel and punishing Yahweh. Like other great Jewish prophets, he sought to reform the religion of his birth, not overthrow it.

By making the bold choice to ride into Jerusalem on the back of a donkey, Jesus symbolized the humility of a worthy leader while making a mockery of the arrogance and greed of prevailing rulers. In the eyes of his enemies, timing the daring, provocative action to coincide with Passover, when thousands of pilgrims were mobbing the streets of Jerusalem, could incite a riot. Jesus' apparent recklessness gave the religious establishment an excuse to be permanently rid of this insurrectionist. In the interest of crowd control, the priests could hand him over to Rome for execution. A famous scene from the classic Broadway musical *Jesus Christ Superstar* portrays the moment of decision with temple priests garbed menacingly in black robes who sing in ominous bass tones: "He is dangerous! He is dangerous!" Therefore, the song goes, "This Jesus must die."

And somewhere between the year 27 and 33, Jesus willingly emptied himself out on a Roman cross to atone for the sins of humankind. But he was reborn within days of his death and has continued to be reborn throughout the ages in the hearts and minds of millions and millions of men and women all over the world. Today over a billion and a half people identify as Christians and look to his teachings for the wisdom of God and salvation.

MARY OF NAZARETH

In the last two Stations of the Light, Mary of Nazareth (Mary the mother of Jesus) emerges as the holy energizing center of the new community that is being born. In the Thirteenth Station with the disciples gathered around her, revering her and sharing her love and faith, she leads them in rapturous prayer of praise while they wait for the spirit of her son to come. Her prayerful, central role continues in the Fourteenth Station, when she and the entire body of followers receive the Pentecostal flames that light the fire of Christ's spirit in their hearts and mystically draw them into the permanent spiritual community of the people of God. Through all those present, but through Mary in a unique way, the fire of love that warms believers' hearts will pass from generation to generation, guiding them to witness to the loving presence of God.

On Pilgrimage with Mary

Mary's entire life is characterized by the modesty of the very poor. She was born into the lowest class of society in a village that was probably populated by families as materially deprived as her own but made secure and strong by their faith and life in a closely knit community. As a female, she received no formal education but, being reared in a devout household of observant Jews, she would have been taught women's traditional responsibilities.

Mary married a woodworker named Joseph and gave birth to a number of sons and daughters, of whom Jesus was the first. We can imagine her working hard to care for her exceptional firstborn. It is difficult to imagine a Middle Eastern woman accustomed to the hard life of the very poor in the timid, passive role to which much religious writing has assigned her. The mother of the Savior was chosen for a work that would exhibit, at its finest, the heart's ability to bear the unbearable, which is courage, not passivity.

From her first appearance in the New Testament, Mary of Nazareth is, like all men and women, on pilgrimage. When we meet her, she is journeying alone over mountains to a village in Judah to be with her cousin Elizabeth while both women are waiting to give birth. Not long after that, we find Mary traveling with Joseph to be counted in the census in Bethlehem, where she unexpectedly gives birth to Jesus. Soon she is under way again, this time going to Jerusalem for Jewish purification rites and to present her child in the temple.

Before long, Mary and her family make a long, arduous journey to Egypt, where they hope to escape Herod's plan to kill male children. When it is safe, they travel back to Nazareth. In addition, as a faithful Jewish woman of her times, Mary must have also made many trips to Jerusalem to fulfill religious duties, such as the annual Feast of Passover.

Her pilgrimage in faith and love is intertwined with the redemptive work of Jesus, whom she knows more intimately than any other person. She raises him, hears him enthrall crowds with the wisdom of God, and witnesses some of the graced and holy moments when he heals or works other signs, as at the wedding of Cana. An anonymous woman in a crowd one day signals that Mary is there by calling out to Jesus: "Blessed the womb that bore you and the breasts that fed you" (Luke 11:27).

Mary's voyage in the physical company of her son culminates in the events of Holy Week and the Easter season, when she walks the Way of the Cross with him through the deepest pain imaginable to the Way of Light and the greatest joy possible.

Mary's Veneration in Islam, Eastern Orthodoxy, and Western Christianity

An Eastern Orthodox story about Mary the mother of Jesus that is not told in the West relates that when she was three years old, she was presented in the temple of Jerusalem and admitted to the holy of holies, which was usually reserved for male priests. She passed a rich childhood there in the company of people dedicated to learning and the pursuit of holiness under the guardianship of the priest Zechariah, who in the Muslim version brought her food only to learn that God had already nourished her. Eastern Orthodoxy preserves the story through a feast day celebrated in the fall.

Islam's sacred scriptures, in the Koran, similarly honor Mary and name an entire chapter for her. Here she is seen as a child whose birth is eagerly awaited, as she is foreseen to have a high destiny serving God's purposes in a special way. Both Eastern Christianity and Islam attribute to Mary youthful wisdom similar to that of Jesus' when he was found in the temple at the age of twelve, suggesting that she stands for almost unlimited holiness, as do, potentially, all pilgrims following in the footsteps of Christ.

In Islam, Eastern Orthodoxy, and Western Christianity, tens of thousands of works of music and art reveal the veneration in which Mary of Nazareth has been held for two thousand years. The Madonna and the figure of mother and child may have inspired more Christians more powerfully than any other images of the divine.

MARY MAGDALENE

Sacred to Jesus

Mary Magdalene is the only person other than Jesus to be honored by more than two stations on the Way of Light: the Second, because she was the first person to learn of the Resurrection; the Third, because she was the first person to whom the risen Lord appeared; and the Fourth, because Jesus chose her above all other disciples to announce the Resurrection and bring humankind hope of eternal life. By singling her out for leadership in the area of the Resurrection, Christianity's most sacred moment, and giving her the authority to speak for him and influence his followers, Jesus recognized her great gifts and worthiness to leave an indelible mark on history.

Not the Repentant Sinner of Luke 7:36–50

Mary Magdalene's reputation as a repentant sinner made her the favorite saint of Teresa of Ávila and endeared her to Hildegard of Bingen, Catherine of Siena, Mother Teresa, and millions of Christians from all walks of life who identify with her. Great works of art contribute to her veneration throughout the West, like Rembrandt's beautiful painting of her meeting

Jesus in the garden, Georges de La Tour's painting of her contemplating a skull, El Greco's *The Repentant Magdalene,* Giotto's *Crucifixion,* and many more. Her feast day has been celebrated on July 22 on the General Roman Calendar since the eighth century, and both Cambridge and Oxford have colleges named after her.

The vastness of her veneration confirms that even people who believed Mary Magdalene was a reformed prostitute identified with the sense of sin she seemed to embody and the sorrow and remorse we feel over doing something wrong. She has always been the saint who inspires repentance.

Ironically, Mary Magdalene was *not* a repentant sinner! This is a later misunderstanding that was absent from the first Christian centuries. The New Testament says only that Jesus "cast out seven demons from her," probably referring to emotional problems that he healed (Mark 16:9). In her own time she was a revered sister-in-the-Lord, loved and admired for her wisdom and devotion, and cherished in Jesus' inner circle because of his high regard for her. She was sacred to Jesus, and early Christians called her "the apostle to the apostles" sent by God to proclaim the Resurrection. Saint Jerome (ca. 345–420) spoke for his era when he described her as a woman of towering strength.

Somehow Mary Magdalene became confused with the repentant woman in Luke 7:36–50 who anointed Jesus, and with Mary of Bethany, who also anointed Jesus (John 11:2).

The misleading idea that Mary Magdalene was a reformed prostitute apparently originated in a fateful sermon (Homily xxxiii), preached on September 14, 591, at the Basilica of Saint Clement in Rome by Saint Gregory the Great, in which he declared her a repentant prostitute. Because this sermon belonged to a homily collection that was widely disseminated and preached in congregations near and far during the next two centuries, the misinterpretation took root in the collective Christian psyche. The myth of that Mary being the repentant sinner of Luke 7:36–50 has prevailed over the truth throughout the last fourteen hundred years and only in our time has begun to be dispelled through the groundbreaking research of scholars like Susan Haskins in her book, *Mary Magdalene.*

The Gospel of Mary

The Gospel of Mary is a noncanonical gospel that was written anonymously "in the spirit of Mary" a century after she lived. The book portrays her as a visionary at the forefront of the Jesus movement who was more insightful than Peter and far more of a visionary than he was. In this text, her enduring mystical experience of communion with the risen Lord makes her a leader in love who comforts and encourages the disciples in the grueling work of building the spiritual community.

Another ancient manuscript rediscovered in the twentieth century, *The Dialogue of the Savior,* presents Mary as the apostle who excels all others. While various manuscripts hint that she may have rivaled Peter for leadership of the Jesus movement for a while, there is no evidence of this in the Christian Scriptures. The fact that a *Gospel of Mary* was written at all, however, and carefully preserved for posterity indicates her immense popularity among Christians in the first and second centuries.

With the exception of Mary the mother of Jesus, Mary Magdalene has exercised more influence in the world than any other woman in Christianity. She was the fountainhead of a great river of spirituality that has flowed throughout the ages century after century, like the powerful Euphrates near her home.

PETER

One of the most beautiful moments on the Way of Light, the Tenth Station, revolves around Peter when Christ charges him with the sacred instruction, "feed my sheep." Peter also is one of the first two men to arrive at the empty tomb and believe in the Resurrection, as well as the first person to enter the tomb, which indicates his natural leadership.

Peter invites half a dozen other men who are similarly great souls to join him in the fishing expedition to the Sea of Tiberias that climaxes with Jesus' cooking breakfast for them. Significantly, this symbolic gesture of "feeding" precedes Jesus' command to Peter to feed his flock. Among the fishermen, whom Jesus is transforming into fishers of people, are Thomas the Twin, Nathanael of Cana, the sons of Zebedee, and two others who remain unnamed.

THOMAS

Another great soul in the Via Lucis is the apostle known as "doubting Thomas," because he exemplifies the need to see and hear with faith. In Station 9, Thomas struggles with doubt until he sees Jesus and hears him speak the words, "Do not be unbelieving, but believing." Thomas is instantaneously enlightened and responds with a passionate confession of faith: "My Lord and my God!"

CLOPAS AND MARY

The Emmaus disciples were traditionally seen as two men, but recent scholarship suggests that the man here, Cleopas (Luke 24:18), is Clopas (John 19:25), the husband of Mary the mother of James and Joses (Mark 15:40). If this is true, then Clopas and Mary, the parents of James and Joses, hold an important place as a married couple in two Stations, the fifth (the road to Emmaus) and the sixth (at the Emmaus inn where Jesus is recognized in the breaking of the bread).

Walking with the risen Lord en route to Emmaus, they are engaged by him in a profound conversation that enables them to be the first of Jesus' followers to understand why he had to die. Their encounter indicates how the prayer of listening and the prayer of conversation with the risen Lord empower Christians of all time to know God and penetrate, at least partially, into deep secrets and mysteries of faith. As the prototype of the Christian pilgrim journeying with God, they have stirred hearts and minds throughout the Christian era.

OTHER PEOPLE ON THE WAY OF LIGHT

In all, there are four women named Mary on the Via Lucis. In addition to Mary the mother of Jesus and Mary Magdalene are Mary of Bethany (the sister of Martha and Lazarus) and Mary the wife of Clopas and the mother of James and Joses. In the tradition of the earliest Gospel, that of Mark, Mary Magdalene and Mary the mother of James and Joses come with a woman named Salome to the empty tomb with bowls of spices and ointments to anoint Jesus' body and are the first to learn of the Resurrection (Mark 16:1–6). Luke adds Joanna and other women (Luke 24:10). John begins with Mary Magdalene and recalls her running to tell Peter and "another disciple" that Jesus is risen (John 20:1–2).

Implicit in the background of the Way of Light is an agrarian local population diversified by inhabitants in the cosmopolitan cities of Galilee. There are Roman soldiers, Arabs, traders from all over the Middle East, and primarily Jews; bearded men, veiled women, and children belonging to families ranging in wealth from the very poor to the truly prosperous. Many languages are heard in the region, such as Hebrew, Greek, Aramaic, Arabic, Coptic, and Latin to name but a few; and educational levels vary widely, with the poor majority being illiterate. Regional religions provide a pantheon of gods and goddesses in addition to Yahweh, the Jewish God.

In springtime of about the year 30, when the events on the Way of Light are unfolding, these diverse people come together in a hilly golden desert with low blue mountains in the distance that can look like burning sand. Fertile green plains are growing lush orchards of date palms, olive and almond trees, mangoes, pomegranates, figs, and oranges. Olive groves shimmer in the sun like water.

Before we journey on the Way of Light with these people in the devotional section of this book, it is helpful to understand how the Way of Light relates to the Way of the Cross, which preceded it by three days. The following chapter explains how the disciples, and we ourselves, make the transition from the Via Crucis to the Via Lucis.

FROM THE STATIONS OF THE CROSS TO THE STATIONS OF THE LIGHT

The Stations of the Cross (Via Crucis) have had a flexible and turbulent history. The number of stations has fluctuated from as few as five to as many as forty-one. The events that the stations commemorate have changed dramatically over time. A few of the scenes have remained at the core of the Via Crucis from the beginning until today, but most of the stations have come and gone over the last two millennia. Nor has the sequence of the various scenes been stable.

In short, very little about the Stations of the Cross has remained static. The devotion apparently has retained its popularity because it responded dynamically to the changing circumstances of different epochs and the changing needs of the people. What most likely started shortly after the crucifixion as a commemoration of Jesus' last day by family, friends, and disciples became in the time of the emperor Constantine the "must-do" pilgrimage to Jerusalem. But for many centuries the pilgrimage remained the province of the well-to-do and deeply devout.

The commemoration of Christ's Passion began to spread from the Middle East to Europe in the twelfth century and accelerated in the next three hundred years. After the Crusades had failed to permanently recapture Jerusalem for Christianity, the Turks took over the Holy Land and the Franciscans were given the responsibility for overseeing the holy places in Palestine.

Today most Roman Catholic churches, many Anglican and Episcopal churches, some other Protestant churches, and the houses of worship of the

Eastern Rite worldwide contain representations of the fourteen Stations of the Cross. The stations are found in Jerusalem along the Via Dolorosa, the Way of Sorrows, and also in gardens and cemeteries and other open-air spaces all over the world. Some of the best-known examples of the Via Crucis are located in the Colosseum in Rome, the Cathedral of Our Lady in Antwerp, Belgium (which includes Rubens's magnificent *Descent from the Cross*), and in Lourdes, France, to name only a very few.

While there was in all likelihood a kind of Via Crucis in Jerusalem from earliest times (though not known by that name until the sixteenth century), there was nothing we know of like it in the West until the early Middle Ages, when Europe began commemorating the final events of the Passion of Christ in one visual way or another. Nothing like today's Stations of the Cross existed anywhere until the eighteenth century. Only in 1731 did Pope Clement XII fix the number of stations at fourteen to commemorate the events that are now called "traditional." The "traditional" stations are a mix of Gospel-based occurrences and scenes steeped in tradition. Half of the "traditional" stations come from the Gospels, mostly Mark and Luke; the other half from cherished church traditions.

In 1975, Pope Paul VI approved a modified, exclusively Gospel-based set of stations. Early in his pontificate, Pope John Paul II suggested adding to the traditional set a fifteenth station, Jesus' Resurrection. At the same time he wrote, and on Good Friday 1991 for the first time prayed, a "new" set of fifteen, strictly Scripture-based stations and offered them to the faithful as an alternative.

· THE "TRADITIONAL" STATIONS OF THE CROSS ·

Here are the "traditional" stations:

Station 1: Pilate condemns Jesus to death (Luke 23:20–25; Mark 15:1–15).

Station 2: Jesus receives the Cross (John 19:17; Mark 15:20).

Station 3: Jesus falls to the ground for the first time.

Station 4: Jesus meets his mother.

Station 5: Simon of Cyrene is obliged to carry the Cross (Mark 15:21; Luke 23:26).

Station 6: Veronica wipes Jesus' face.

Station 7: Jesus falls a second time.

Station 8: Jesus talks to the women of Jerusalem (Luke 23:27–31).

Station 9: Jesus falls a third time.

Station 10: Jesus is stripped of his garments.

Station 11: Jesus is nailed to the cross (Mark 15:22–26; Luke 23:32–34).

Station 12: Jesus dies on the cross (Matthew 27:45–50; Mark 15:33–37).

Station 13: Jesus' body is taken down from the cross.

Station 14: Jesus' body is placed in the tomb (Matthew 27:57–61; Mark 15:46).

· THE "NEW" STATIONS OF THE CROSS ·

Here are the Stations of the Cross as recommended by Pope John Paul II, including fifteenth station:

1. Jesus prays in the Garden of Olives (Luke 22:39–42, 45–46; Mark 14:33–36).

2. Jesus is betrayed by Judas (Matthew 26:45–49; Mark 14:43, 44–46).

3. Jesus is condemned by the Sanhedrin (Mark 14:55–56, 60–65).

4. Jesus is denied by Peter (Luke 22:54–62; Mark 14:66–72).

5. Jesus is judged by Pilate (Luke 23:20–25; Mark 15:1–15).

6. Jesus is scourged and crowned with thorns (John 19:1–3; Mark 15:15–20).

7. Jesus carries his cross (John 19:17; Mark 15:20).

8. Jesus is helped by Simon of Cyrene (Mark 15:20–21; Luke 23:26).
9. Jesus encounters the women of Jerusalem (Luke 23:27–31).
10. Jesus is crucified (Mark 15:22–26; Luke 23:32–34).
11. Jesus promises to share his reign with the good thief (Luke 23:39–43).
12. Jesus is on the cross, with his mother and disciples below (John 19:25–27; Luke 23:34–35).
13. Jesus dies on the cross (Matthew 27:45–50; Mark 15:33–37).
14. Jesus is placed in the tomb (Matthew 27:57–61; Mark 15:46).
15. Holy Saturday and Easter Resurrection (Luke 24:1–3).

The Stations of the Cross in Jerusalem

In Jerusalem the "traditional" Stations of the Cross have remained stable since the late 1800s. Today's stations and the route of the Via Dolorosa along which they are located have of course been bent by the realities of Christian and Muslim strife and history, the imperfect memory of "experts" and pilgrims, and the needs and possibilities of the Franciscans.

It is likely that even immediately after the crucifixion the precise location of each event of Jesus' walk to Golgotha was not universally accepted. Eyewitnesses of the same events notoriously disagree on many details. What is more, in A.D. 70 the city of Jerusalem was razed by the Romans and again in A.D. 135, each time after the latest Jewish revolt was cruelly put down. After A.D. 135 the Romans built a new city on the ruins of Jerusalem and raised a pagan shrine on the Temple Hill. Only in A.D. 326, nearly three hundred years after Jesus' crucifixion, did Helena, Emperor Constantine's Christian mother, designate, on scant and controversial evidence, some of the major sites of Jesus' Passion. In the seventeen hundred years since then, Persians, Crusaders, Arabs, and Seljuk Turks, to mention only a few, have warred over the city, destroyed it, rebuilt it, and obviously buried the faint traces of the physical Jesus more and more. When the Franciscans became the guardians of the holy places in the area, they had to make accommodations with the Turks and create a route that was both reasonably safe and accessible to the average pilgrim. From this mélange has emerged today's Via Dolorosa.

The Via Crucis begins where Herod Antipas's Antonia Fortress, a stronghold that overlooked the Temple Mount from the north and where the Roman soldiers were garrisoned, stood at one time. This is the likeliest place where Pontius Pilate would have taken residence while in Jerusalem. (His usual residence was in Caesarea; only for the high Jewish holidays did the Roman procurator come to Jerusalem to keep the peace.) Here he condemned Jesus to death. In 1920 the Church of the Flagellation was built on this site. This is the First Station.

The Second Station, where Jesus received the Cross, is located near the remains of a Roman triumphal arch, now named the Arch of Ecce Homo, which itself for a long time was a station of the Via Crucis. The center part of the structure spans the Via Dolorosa while one of the side arches has been incorporated into the Chapel of the Ecce Homo in the Convent of the Sisters of Zion.

A small chapel, built in the nineteenth century and belonging to the Armenian Catholic patriarchate, marks the Third Station, where Jesus is said to have fallen for the first time under the weight of the cross. During World War II the chapel was renovated and completed by Catholic soldiers of the Free Polish Army.

A small Armenian oratory commemorates the place where Jesus meets his mother. This is the Fourth Station of the Cross.

At the Fifth Station, the faithful are reminded of Simon of Cyrene, who helps Jesus carry the cross. A Franciscan chapel has been built to mark the site.

Veronica is remembered at the Sixth Station, the site where she is said to have wiped Jesus' face. A small church stands at the location now.

A Franciscan chapel indicates the Seventh Station, where Jesus is said to have fallen for the second time.

The Eighth Station is a small cross carved into the wall of a Greek Orthodox monastery and indicates the place where Jesus spoke to the women of Jerusalem.

A column from the Roman period at the entrance to the Coptic Monastery of Saint Anthony signals the Ninth Station, where Jesus is said to have fallen for the third time.

The final five stations are inside the Church of the Holy Sepulchre, where the hill of Golgotha once rose. The original Holy Sepulchre was built on the site in 326 by Helena, Constantine's mother, destroyed by the Persians in 614, rebuilt by the Byzantines in 1086, destroyed by the Muslims in 1099, and then modified, razed, and newly erected by the Crusaders between 1099 and 1149. It remained more or less intact until 1808 when fire destroyed most of it. Greek monks rebuilt it yet again, but with significant changes.

The Chapel of the Crucifixion designates the place where Jesus was stripped of his garments (the Tenth Station of the Cross) and nailed to the cross (the Eleventh Station). The Twelfth Station, "Jesus dies on the Cross," is commemorated by the Chapel of Calvary. While the Chapel of the Crucifixion belongs to the Roman Catholic Church, the Greek Orthodox Church owns the Chapel of Calvary.

The Stone of Unction marks the place where, according to tradition, Jesus' body was laid and anointed after he was brought down from the cross.

The Shrine of the Holy Sepulchre is located in the middle of the Rotunda of Anastasis over an ancient tomb, where it is believed Jesus' body lay from Good Friday to Easter Sunday. This is the Fourteenth Station.

◆　◆　◆

As far as we know, virtually nothing is recorded about the specific sites of Jesus' Passion for a few hundred years while the institutional church was building and enduring bitter persecutions in the Roman Empire. In 312 the Western Roman emperor, Constantine, had a vision and a dream exhorting him to fight under the sign of the cross of the Christians. In this vision, he and his entire army, in broad daylight, saw a cross appear in the heavens above the sun. Constantine alone saw an inscription urging him to fight under the sign of this cross in the future. When a powerful dream repeated the instructions, he decided to follow the guidance and won a crucial battle against his rival for the emperorship at the Milvian Bridge, a few miles outside of Rome. Because of this victory, he became the undisputed emperor of the Western half of the Roman Empire.

A few months later, in 313, Constantine promulgated the Edict of Milan, granting freedom of worship to Christians. The edict declared: "We resolve to grant both to the Christians and to all men freedom to follow the religion which they choose, that whatever heavenly divinity exists may be propitious to us and to all who live under our government."

Helena, Constantine's mother, who had become a devout Christian under her son's influence, made a pilgrimage to the Holy Land in 326. In Jerusalem she endeavored to locate and commemorate the sites of Jesus' life and in many instances caused churches and chapels to be built at these locations. It inaugurated a prosperous and splendid epoch for Jerusalem and its environs that lasted under the protection of the Byzantine emperors until first the Persians and then the Muslim Arabs conquered the city in the seventh century.

Saint Jerome in the early fifth century spoke of the crowds of pilgrims that visited the city to see and worship at the sites of Christ's sufferings. On the other hand, in about A.D. 380 a traveler and writer by the name of Sylvia, in her *Peregrinatio ad loca sancta (Pilgrimage to the Holy Land)*, does not even mention a Via Crucis–style devotion in Jerusalem, although she describes minutely every other religious exercise that she saw practiced in the city and its surroundings.

The earliest attested attempt, and an isolated one for another six to seven hundred years, to represent some of the holy sites of Jerusalem elsewhere, dates to the fifth century. Saint Petronius, bishop of Bologna, ordered the construction at the monastery and church of San Stefano five connected chapels that represented some of the most important shrines of Jerusalem.

In 1095, in response to pleas for help from the Christian Byzantine emperor against the Muslim Seljuk Turks, Pope Urban II at the Council of Clermont called for a holy war to reconquer Jerusalem and the Holy Land. For nearly two hundred years Western Christians invaded the Holy Land, fought over it, ruled it, and eventually lost it.

While there was a Via Sacra (a Sacred Way) along which pilgrims were conducted in the centuries of the Crusades and even thereafter, it seemed to bear little resemblance to the Stations of the Cross as we know them to-day. The great German mystic Henry Suso (1300–1366) may have been the spiritual originator of the Stations of the Cross. He described his own "spiritual pilgrimage" as following Jesus step-by-step in his imagination while meditating on the Passion of Christ.

In 1342, Pope Clement VI committed the holy places in Palestine to the care of the Franciscans. The Order saw it as one of its missions to promote the Stations of the Cross as a devotion, and they have done so ever since. Beginning with their arrival in the Holy Land and through all the vicissitudes of repression and necessary accommodations—first with the Mamelukes, then with the Ottomans, and finally in light of the contemporary Jewish/Palestinian conflict—the Franciscans have built and retained a Way of the Cross. If their Via Crucis is not historically accurate, spiritually it is deeply satisfying.

◆   ◆   ◆

After the Crusades and particularly in the fifteenth and sixteenth centuries, when it became more and more difficult to make pilgrimages to the Holy Land because of the more severe restrictions imposed first by the Mamelukes and then the Ottomans, reproductions of the principal scenes of Christ's Passion began to appear in Europe. Veterans of the Crusades had brought back relics and memories of the places where Jesus lived and died. They had started to construct Stations of the Cross, although not yet called that and certainly not what we have today. The Franciscans' promotion of the Stations of the Cross had an effect all across Europe because of the Order's numbers and influence.

The Blessed Alvarez, a Dominican friar, on his return from the Holy Land around 1400, built a series of little chapels at the Dominican friary of Cordova, Spain. In each was painted a particular event commemorating Jesus' suffering. Sometime after 1450, the Blessed Eustochia (ca. 1434–ca. 1486), a Poor Clare of Assisi, constructed a set of stations at her convent in Messina, Sicily. In about 1465 a burgher by the name of G. Emmerich erected stations in Goerlitz, near Breslau, which was then the far edge of the German world.

William Wey, an English pilgrim who visited the Holy Land in 1458 and again in 1462, apparently was the first, though, to use the word "stations" for the stopping places along the Via Sacra in Jerusalem. He may also have been the first traveler to report that pilgrims progressed from Pontius Pilate's house to Mount Calvary. Until that time, the pilgrimage apparently had been made in reverse, from Calgary to Pilate's house. There are other reports that the Way of the Cross was not normally walked in the "correct" direction until the Franciscan friar Saint Leonard of Port Maurice reestablished the practice in the early 1700s.

Over the centuries the number of stations has varied widely, from five to forty-two. Wey's list from 1458 mentions fourteen stations, but only five correspond to today's. Romanet Bofin, another pilgrim who built stations in Europe, in 1515 was told by two friars in Jerusalem that there were thirty-one stations. The Manuals of Devotion of the time, however, variously listed nineteen, twenty-five, and thirty-seven stations.

In fact, these stations were not at all the stations that the Franciscans were showing to the faithful pilgrims in Jerusalem at the same time, nor did they reflect the carefully written guidebooks to the stations that the Franciscans were publishing.

Martin Ketzel, a prominent merchant from Nurenburg, Germany, made a pilgrimage to Jerusalem in the late 1400s and not only selected his seven favorite scenes from Christ's passion but also measured the distance between each. On his way home all his carefully wrapped notes and measurements went overboard in a storm in the Mediterranean, and Ketzel had to return to Jerusalem to pace out the distances again. Upon his return to Nurenburg, he commissioned the city's well-known master carver, Adam Kent, to create seven Stations of the Cross, which became popularly known as the "Seven Falls of Christ." Today one can make out at the base of each carving what it represents.

Apparently the needs and desires of the people contributed as much as the desires of church officials to the shaping of the Stations of the Cross as we know them today. When Pope Clement XII declared in 1731 that there would be fourteen Stations of the Cross and what would be commemorated at each, it is likely he was approving what tradition had already decided.

Today the Via Crucis remains one of the most popular devotions in the Roman Catholic and Eastern Rite Churches, particularly during Lent.

The idea of a Way of Light undoubtedly arose very early. Immediately after the Crucifixion and Resurrection, the disciples must have wanted to retrace Jesus' last steps to reflect on the meaning of his life and death. Considering the animosity of the Sanhedrin to Jesus' followers and the Roman desire to maintain order, they would have needed to be very circumspect. But the custom of revisiting the sites where Jesus suffered undoubtedly became a spiritual practice very early in the first century. Whether or not Christians also visited the sites of the Way of Light remains a matter for conjecture or archaeological discovery, but it is unlikely that events as crucial to the Christian story as the Resurrection, ascension, and Pentecost would have been omitted from the pilgrimage.

Roman Catholic tradition recounts that Mary the mother of Jesus went to the sites of her son's suffering every day. Probably the earliest written record of her visits comes from a Syriac manuscript of the fifth century. Based on it, an eminent nineteenth-century German biblical scholar published the following account of Mary's pilgrimages:

> When the apostles had separated in order to preach the gospel and had traveled to different parts of the world, the blessed Virgin . . . is said to have remained in Jerusalem. . . . Thence, as long as she lived, she used to visit every spot which her Son's presence had sanctified, the place . . . of his passion, resurrection and ascension.

What is fascinating about this statement is the reference to the Resurrection and ascension, two events that take place on the Way of the Light, not the Way of the Cross. Although there is no solid historical evidence for Mary's pilgrimages to the locations associated with her son's crucifixion and Resurrection, it makes sense that a mother would have made such visits. And it is likely that the visits would have included not only the places where he suffered and died, but also the locations where he reappeared and gave some of his most beautiful and joyful teachings, the Via Lucis.

The next chapter returns to the topic of the Way of Light to consider some of the many spiritual gifts we receive from praying the Stations of the Light.

GIFTS OF THE
WAY OF LIGHT

Here are some of the blessings, the delights, and the spiritual gifts that come to you from practicing the Way of Light:

· A JOYFUL SPIRITUALITY ·

Try this: Place a small container of soil on a sunny windowsill and bury a seed in it from an orange, tomato, lemon, lime, apple, or any fruit or vegetable you happen to have in your kitchen. Then wait and see what happens. Give the earth a little water when it dries, and chances are that you will soon be surprised and rewarded by joy.

Something similar happens when we practice the Stations of the Light. Each of us has a small seed of the divine embedded at the center of our bodies that needs only a little tending to open and grow into something beautiful. And amazingly, the sacred process never ends. It is as though the original divine seed was always there, opening and reopening, giving birth over and over as long as we live. All we are asked to do is trust the interplay of darkness and light and give the seed a little help by keeping the soil moist and saying "yes" to the grace of the moment.

The Way of Light is a spirituality of joy because praying the stations leads to growth and amazing surprises. Even when we use the practices to get through a difficult time, they release a lightheartedness and gladness to be alive from a space in the soul that is deeper than feelings, thoughts, and images. Each exercise seeks to be exhilarating by reinforcing the clear New Testament teaching that spiritual life is an invitation to maximize joy despite deep pain. Saint Anselm of Canterbury said it well some ten centuries ago: "I have known a joy that is *full,* and *more* than full," meaning that the depth and breadth of joy that we receive in the spiritual journey surpasses even our greatest expectations.

As you progress from station to station on the Way of Light, you may notice an evolution of joy from early glimmers of it to rapture. At the beginning of Station 1, before anyone learns of the Resurrection, there is a sense of the deep grief experienced by Christ's loved ones in the face of his harrowing execution and subsequent disappearance of his body. The psychic state of the first person we meet, the especially beloved disciple Mary Magdalene, is desolation, but that desolation is short-lived. Immediately angels, whose very being symbolizes bliss, descend from the heavens to seed the Way of Light with joy by announcing the Resurrection. By the time you reach the Third Station, Christ has reappeared and makes himself known to Mary in a moving scene that causes her heart to burst open with love. When he sends her to share the news with his disciples, it is not difficult to imagine her happiness soaring—like our own when we share a beautiful experience with a friend, and the beauty is magnified.

When we reach the Fifth and Sixth Stations, two more disciples, Cleopas and Mary, the parents of James and Joses, meet Jesus on the road to Emmaus, and their hearts virtually catch on fire with wonder and awe as he teaches them the meaning of his life and death. Before long, Jesus appears to a large number of his followers in the Upper Room, and we feel a spirit of soaring, contagious joy overtaking the entire room. The progression continues, swells, warms, and by the time we arrive at the Thirteenth Station, "Waiting with Mary in the Upper Room," the exultation is building toward the great culmination of the Way of Light on Pentecost in an explosion of wisdom and bliss. The whole community is gathered around Mary, raising their hearts "in one voice" of prayer praising God, and just when we feel there can be no greater joy than this great song of praise, the

Fourteenth Station brings us to the fiery descent of the Spirit of Christ over the community, lifting everyone into a state of sheer ecstasy.

Joy evolves through the fourteen Stations of the Light like a contagion, passing from person to person, growing in strength and intensity, unveiling divine purposes, motivating the community to persevere in the life of prayer. Part of the teaching of the Way of Light is that joy is so integral to Christian spirituality that it belongs close to the "theological virtues" of faith, hope, and love. The very pattern of the Christian believer's life includes joy, as Jesus taught his disciples with the following words: "These things I have spoken to you, that my joy may be in you, and that your joy may be full" (John 15:11).

The greatest gift of the Way of Light is itself, precisely because it is a joyful spirituality.

· CONTEMPLATIVE LIVING ·

The Way of Light offers opportunities for both introverted spiritual practice and extroverted creativity, which together form the basis of contemplative living, meaning awareness or mindfulness in the moment. The word "contemplation" comes from the Latin word for "temple" and the prefix "with," which loosely translates as "being with God in a temple." The very opposite of materialism, a contemplative life functions as greed-prevention and is the one antidote we have to consumerism. Because spirituality adds dimensions of wakefulness, silence, and solitude to our lives, our desires shift away from wanting to have or possess and instead move toward wanting greater contentment, or more precisely, toward being content with who, where, and what we are.

In the process of living contemplatively, our values change. Thoughtful communication can become more important than just talking, sensitivity to the people around us can come to outweigh self-absorption, and the way things really are can matter more than appearances or prestige.

Paradoxically, by turning inward we turn outward. Concentrated attention on the inner life always eventually results in increased receptivity to others and compassion for the plight of the world, both ecologically and politically. In the Christian Scriptures, the Greek word for the process of turning outward after a time of inwardness, *exousia,* denotes an important work of the spirit in the individual soul.

Zen master Doc The has a lovely poem about contemplative living that also illustrates what it is like when attention shifts to the huge world of need beyond ourselves, a value cherished in every religion:

> *While buttoning my jacket*
> *I hope that all beings*
> *Will keep their hearts warm*
> *And not lose themselves.*

A similar practice from the Christian mystical tradition invites us when dressing to say a prayer for the anonymous persons involved in making each aspect of our clothing, from weaving the cloth to sewing the last seam.

When we first decide to undertake a more contemplative lifestyle and sit down to meditate silently, most of us find our inner stream of thoughts jumping from association to association wildly, unfocused and directionless. For this reason, Eastern religions compare the human thought-stream to monkeys swinging from branch to branch in the jungle and call the untrained mind the "monkey mind." Calming the mind is a first goal of meditation and of the Way of Light.

At the heart of Christianity's approach to contemplative spirituality is the practice of the presence of God, which takes many forms and also for some people is a way to follow Saint Paul's apparently demanding teaching to "pray always." Brother David Steindl-Rast, author of *Gratefulness: The Heart of Prayer*, tells the story of an elderly couple who devised a very beautiful practice to meet both purposes. All day long when the clock strikes the hour, the husband quietly says: "It is —— o'clock," and the wife replies, "Let us remember the presence of God." The retired Episcopal bishop John Shelby Spong created another unique practice for the same reasons. He painted a small cross over the face of his wristwatch to remind himself of God's presence every time he checked the time.

As the mind becomes more still throughout the months and years of practice, we begin to reap the treasures of silence, first, paradoxically, by hearing beautiful new sounds or sounds we may not have heard in a very long time. The late writer and priest Henri Nouwen describes "the sounds of silence" poetically:

> Silence is full of sounds. The wind murmuring, the leaves rustling, the birds flapping their wings, the waves washing ashore. And even if these sounds cannot be heard, we still hear our own quiet breathing, the motion of our hand over our skin, the swallowing of our throats, and the soft patter of our footsteps.

Continuing in contemplative living leads us from these early sounds of silence to the even more precious gift of new dimensions of life and soul-mysteries.

Pure silence may seem inaccessible, like the space between breaths or between the notes in a song, yet we eventually do receive experiences of it, which have powerful effects. When we sit down to our spiritual practice session stressed by the chaos all around us, feeling fragile, or confused about who we are and what we are supposed to be doing, only a few minutes of quiet can restore the peace and happiness of contemplative life.

· PEACE AND HAPPINESS ·

The Dalai Lama, whose personal spiritual practice includes smiling whenever he enters a room, incarnates in his own loving presence what he understands by the word happiness. From his spiritual point of view, happiness is a "peaceful state of essential openness and compassion," meaning that happiness is not the gaudy emotion seen in advertisements but is rather the natural way for us to feel and to be. Happiness is "a warm inner state," and it is as visible on our own faces as on the face of the Dalai Lama when we allow prayer and meditation to relax the body, open the heart, and unclutter the mind from disturbing thoughts and worries. This is the simplest way to be happy, to enjoy our innate and natural state of inner warmth while making the effort to prevent "cold inner states" like anger, aggression, and cynicism.

The Christian Scriptures say that "There is nothing better for us than to be happy" (Ecclesiastes 3:12). Scientific tests in the West have verified this, unintentionally confirming what Buddhists, Hindus, and people of other Eastern religions have always believed: that negative emotions can raise blood pressure, respiration, cortisol, and other stress hormones to unhealthy levels, while positive feelings can drop these levels to normal. Nurturing positive emotions such as kindness, tenderness, gentleness, affection, and friendliness is conducive to better health—our own and that of the people around us. Negative emotions such as anger, resentment, jealousy, and mean-spiritedness have harmful effects on health. Taking up the Dalai Lama's practice of smiling every time we enter a room undoubtedly could bring many blessings to others and to ourselves.

It is more effective spiritually to cultivate positive mental states and think positively than to fight negativity, which increases tension and stress. Today there is knowledge of the brain's plasticity, meaning its ability to change structurally throughout a lifetime in response to behavioral changes. Cognitive psychology shows that changing our thinking causes structural changes in the brain detectable in an MRI. In other words, there is hard evidence that the harmful effects of biochemical changes produced during negative mental or emotional states are prevented by positive thinking and behavior. Mind-body clinics and meditation halls based on these principles teach tension-release techniques of healing through the cultivation of positive mental and emotional states—which is a good argument for doing what we enjoy doing insofar as it is possible. Part of everyone's life calls for doing some things we do not enjoy.

The Way of Light, as a positive, welcoming spirituality, conduces to warm and healthy inner states while encouraging us to let go of the coldness and suffering caused by negative thoughts and feelings. Exercises for the Way of Light intentionally foster the joyful use of imagination and creativity to help bring us back, when we lose our way, to the fundamental human state of peaceful, outward-looking, caring, receptive happiness in which we are born. Saint Paul points to the problem of negative thinking by urging the congregation at Philippi to think about positive things to find peace: "Whatever is true, whatever is honorable, whatever is just, whatever is pure, whatever is lovely, whatever is gracious, where there is excellence, where there is anything worthy of praise, think about these things." If you use your mind this way, Paul promises the Philippians, and follow Jesus' teachings, "the God of peace will be with you" (Philippians 4:8–9).

Paul also mentions that he has learned to be content with whatever life sends him, whether he likes it or not, although he—like the lighthearted Dalai Lama—has suffered severe persecution and hardship: "I know how to be put down, and I know how to be raised up; in any and all circumstances, I have learned the secret of facing plenty and hunger, abundance and lack." The secret lies in the God who is always with him, ready to strengthen him. He is happy, he has made the effort. Much of it is his own doing, but much is due to the grace of God.

Sikh spiritual teachers have been known to include laughter as a five-minute exercise in a yoga class. Seated cross-legged on a mat like the students, the teacher starts laughing with unbridled delight while the contagion passes throughout the room to one student after another until the whole room has erupted in hilarity. Students leave the class in high spirits and with a memorable experience of easy access to the warm and positive inner state of happiness.

· LOVE ·

It is love that prayer kindles in the soul. Practicing the Way of Light is like digging a hole to plant a bush and discovering an amazing underground river of love that never recedes from its banks and never runs dry, since it has its source in an infinite source of replenishment. Different kinds of love can be discerned like individual streams in the river that range from the intimacy and self-disclosure in friendship to mystical feelings of intense devotion to God. Since all these forms of love originate in the Source of Life, they are all connections in goodness, like friendship, compassion, and mystical love.

Romantic love, for all its delights and excitements, is the one form of love absent from the Way of Light, although the myth of an erotic attachment between Jesus and Mary Magdalene surfaces from time to time throughout history, as again in our own time in a popular novel. There is no evidence of any kind to support such a myth. What is known, though, is that the deep love that connects Mary Magdalene to Jesus combines elements of friendship and mystical love. It could be called "erotic" in the original meaning of the word "erotic," which comes from the name of the Greek god Eros, who is more a god of connection rather than of romance. Eros denotes the mysterious attracting force that brings people together into all kinds of relationships.

· FRIENDSHIP ·

On the Way of Light, friendship is one of the most important energies that enable the Christian story to unfold according to plan. As friendship plays a similar role in our own lives, helping our personal Christian stories to develop, it is wise to look to the stations for models. There are many degrees and forms of friendship represented in the stations that can serve as models for our own.

The finest example is, of course, the unconditional friendship Jesus offers his followers without exception, even when they betray him (like Judas) or deny knowing him (like Peter) and prove themselves virtually incapable of reciprocating his love. While Jesus' behavior toward them is based on self-transcendence, freedom, commitment, and promises that will be kept, the friendship they show him is weak and unreliable, ego-centered, and hot or cold depending on fluctuating emotions. At least, that is, until the end of the Way of Light when the Holy Spirit illumines the disciples' minds and hearts and brings them together in a community. After that, they are all willing to give to others what Jesus gave them, to "spend and be spent" for his sake (2 Corinthians 12:15), and even to die for him, as will Stephen and Peter to name but two.

At the time of Jesus' death, most of his disciples disconnect from him. Judas and Peter behave the worst while others run away in fear for their lives. That negative pattern belongs to the Way of the Cross, however. On the Way of Light, friendship undergoes a remarkable development that models a path to maturity for our own relationships. What makes the difference? How is it possible that the ordinary people Jesus selected as his companions, who abandon him on the Via Crucis, become exemplars of the fullness of friendship and sacrificial love on the Via Lucis? What empowers cowardly Peter to grow into a heroic, self-giving sage?

The disciples' transformation, like our own, begins with the First Station of Light, the Resurrection, and develops over the course of the next thirteen stations. In the Eighth Station, for instance, the disciples learn how to forgive, a central ingredient of friendship. The Ninth Station reinforces faith, another component of a solid bond. The Tenth provides a magnificent teaching about how to love, without which friendship dies. In the Thirteenth Station, praying with Mary in the Upper Room, the disciples are given the fullest experience imaginable of the joy that issues from prayer, and at Pentecost, the closing station, they receive the Spirit of God.

This far-reaching journey in Christian spirituality mirrors our own incomplete voyages, and the Way of Light showers grace on us at every step to help us stay on the path all the way to the end. An eighty-eight-year-old man was overheard to remark that "in the eighties, everyone is a friend." He was making the point that when time begins running out and heaven seems close, the criteria of friendship loosen substantially. There is no more time to be judgmental, intolerant, or rejecting, no more time to waste in ego games. Every relationship in elderhood is precious, and every person is a gift. Happily, spiritual practice takes us toward that blessed state of contentment long before the eighties, if we wish. Saint Thomas Aquinas taught his students that the very goal of ethics is friendship, and one of the gifts of the Way of Light is the discovery of how much friendship means, and how simple it is to be a friend.

Perhaps because we become more awake and focused by doing the practices, we almost automatically become more responsive to our friends, more caring about their situations and needs.

· FAMILY BONDS ·

One of the most moving stories in the New Testament is that of the heart-broken couple* walking along the road to Emmaus, trying to understand why their beloved Teacher was just put to death. This archetypal scene is usually interpreted in terms of human existence and the spiritual journey, but it also offers a rich image of marriage based in loving and thoughtful communication and shared experience. The travelers, Mary and Clopas, the parents of James and Joses, walk side by side in the same direction, sometimes looking ahead, presumably, and sometimes looking at each other as they communicate deeply about the things that matter most in life. (Little has been written on this splendid image of the journey in marriage or partnership, which should be lifted up as a model for couples and also friends.)

Before long, a wise and comforting stranger who turns out to be the risen Lord comes along and helps them understand the mystery that is preoccupying them. Here is a timeless image of a married couple connected to each other in the mysterious spiritual presence that grounds their relationship and gives it direction and meaning. It is as though they are living beyond themselves, beyond the ego's personal agendas, for something larger than their own lives. A mutually supportive and fulfilling partnership is implicit in the scene.

At dusk the setting changes to a dinner table at an inn where the Emmaus couple invite the risen Lord to break bread with them. The meal begins with a blessing that hints at the Last Supper and the Eucharist, then

---

*The Emmaus disciples were traditionally seen as two men, but recent scholarship suggests that the man here, Cleopas (Luke 24:18), is Clopas (John 19:25), the husband of Mary the mother of James and Joses (Mark 15:40).

Jesus disappears, leaving the couple to deepen and grow together in the mysteries he has disclosed.

The two scenes are commemorated in the Fifth and Sixth Stations, respectively, which contain practices suitable for the whole family to share or do separately and then discuss over dinner. We can imagine Mary and Clopas arriving home to a large extended family including grandparents and young children and saying a blessing together before the meal. A family that has been inspired by Jesus' teachings will perpetuate his guidance and values at home.

Praying the Way of Light inspires parents to model Mary and Clopas's example of thoughtful communication with each other and passionate caring about divine mystery. It is a combination of Jesus' teachings and grace that empowers them to bring out the best soul-qualities in one another and in those around them. One gift of the Way of Light in this area could be noticing where we need to do some work on ourselves in relationship to the family. Would more thoughtful communication help? Or would it be best to more consciously imitate Jesus (or Mary, his mother)?

· COMPASSION ·

Compassion, which comes from two Latin words meaning "feeling with" another person, is one of the most important forms of love inspired by the Stations of the Light, especially the Tenth Station, where Jesus gives Peter his ultimate teaching on compassion through the metaphor of a shepherd taking care of his sheep. Christians, in particular American Christians, are extremely generous with time and resources given in service to the poor and in volunteer programs for literally hundreds of causes. Twelve-step groups alone serve over 140 different causes.

Much of the West's motivation to "care" comes from moving stories in the Gospels, for example, Jesus' stories about finding something or someone who is lost, quenching hunger and thirst, welcoming strangers, clothing the poor, and visiting the sick and prisoners. These stories have moved men and women to take radical action on behalf of others because, as Christ said, "In so far as you did it to one of the least of these my brothers or sisters," he says, "you did it to me" (Matthew 25:40).

Angels, as messengers to humankind, symbolize divine compassion in the First Station with the message, "Do not be afraid" (Matthew 28:5), and reappear for a similar purpose in the Twelfth. The grace of a spiritual antidote to fear grows in us over time while practicing the Way of Light.

Today, no spiritual gift is more needed than compassion in wealthy Western countries, like most of the European nations and the United States, where desperately poor immigrants and refugees from all over the world seek sanctuary from despair and wars. Christians in privileged nations are called to honor these new brothers and sisters by welcoming the diversity of faces, languages, traditions, and religions as a blessing of new energy and creativity for the host country as well as a sacred opportunity for us to lighten the burdens of the poor. Just as the risen Lord walks a dusty desert road with the Emmaus couple, so is he with the suffering people who enter the United States and Europe, legally and illegally. Welcoming immigrants and refugees begins in the heart's innate compassion, which recognizes, when it is unblocked by selfishness, what acute suffering drives men and women to leave their homes and brave an unknowable future in a sometimes-rejecting foreign country.

Another issue of diversity that calls for compassion in the United States pertains to the immigration of Catholics. Most American Catholics use the Roman rite and are called Roman Catholic, while most Catholics coming into the country are Eastern Orthodox and use the Eastern rite. Significant differences, such as a married clergy in the Eastern tradition, pose potential barriers. In addition, Catholic immigrants from South America tend to be evangelical, and those from Africa may combine ancient indigenous traditions with the Catholic liturgy. Ongoing spiritual practice enables us to interpret the changes positively as a wonderfully diversified and enriched matrix for a stimulating cross-fertilization of ideas and rituals.

As Jesus taught, ". . . love one another; as I have loved you" (John 13:34).

· SPIRITUAL EXPERIENCE ·

Sylvia Boorstein, who teaches Buddhist meditation at Spirit Rock, a spiritual center in the golden hills outside San Francisco, described a spiritual experience that took place during meditation. It comes from her book, *That's Funny, You Don't Look Buddhist:* "In the middle of a Buddhist meditation retreat" she writes, "my mind filled with a peace I had not known before—completely restful, balanced, alert, joyous peace—and I said *'Baruch Hashem'* " (Praise God).

Sylvia Boorstein's uncomplicated experience of peace typifies the quality of spiritual experience that every meditator ultimately (or sometimes instantly) meets with. Her story illustrates also, however indirectly, that the discipline of spiritual practice is necessary for us to reach our experiential spiritual potential, full use of the powers of the soul. If only for five minutes a day, a steady, committed practice is a prerequisite to open a channel for grace to flow into the heart and ready us for ever brighter and more beautiful adventures in spirituality.

Spiritual experience is strengthening because it dissipates doubts about the invisible world and reaffirms the unconditional promise that sorrow always eventually turns into joy. It also enables us to look at strong unpleasant emotions (like fear) and dangerous emotions (say anger and self-pity) from the point of view of the larger self who knows how to relate to negative emotion wisely. In addition, the wonder, beauty, and bliss in spiritual experience unveils astounding capacities in the soul that reinforce and expand our longing for inner warmth and natural distaste for the cold emotions.

For some people, a single spiritual experience gives them a memory that will last for a lifetime. Others have a thinner veil and more frequent connections with God. Still others avoid spiritual experience completely for fear of losing control. These latter people need to know, and will learn by practicing the Way of Light, that letting go of control is the path par excellence to all the beauties and mysteries of spirituality.

"Mystical" experience differs from "spiritual" experience only in being more intense, a passageway to directly encountering the living God, as when Mechtild of Magdeburg in thirteenth-century Germany saw "the flowing light of the Godhead."

The Way of Light is from beginning to end a path of mystical experience. A dead man comes back to life; angels manifest; people have visions; flames set spirits on fire; there is continual contact with God through the risen Christ; the Holy Spirit is seen to descend on humans in flames; and the highest form of love, mystical love, is released in men's and women's hearts. Three words that the New Testament uses interchangeably for "God," which all happen to begin with the letter *L*, are explicit or implicit at every station: love, life, and light. Christian, Hindu, Sufi, and other religions' mystical writings contain a storehouse of experiences where all three come together, as in the following vision of a very illumined soul, Saint Hildegard of Bingen, whom the sacred Scriptures nourished from earliest childhood in fertile, light-filled symbols and images, many of which are found on the Way of Light. In the following vision, God speaks:

> I, the fiery Life of Divine essence, flame in the beauty of the meadows. I gleam in the waters. I burn in the sun, moon, and stars. With every breeze, as with invisible life that embraces everything, I awaken all creatures to life. . . . I am the breeze that nurtures all things green. I encourage blossoms to flourish with ripening fruits; I am the rain coming from the dew that causes the grasses to laugh with the joy of life.

Hildegard's vision of the divine shining in creation expresses the same "burning" love that the Emmaus couple mentions in Station 6, only in a more intense and poetic form. It suggests also the paradisal garden of Stations 3 and 4, where Mary Magdalene meets the living Christ. It is reminiscent, too, of the Fourteenth Station, when the Pentecostal Spirit of Christ streams down on the disciples, imparting the gift of tongues.

The content of mystical or spiritual experience is always symbolic, and it is wise to always ask yourself what each symbol means, what it has come to teach you, what you need to learn.

· REVERENCE FOR THE SACRED ·

The pilgrim within each of us who loves the beauty, surprises, rhythms, and cycles of nature throughout the four seasons knows the meaning of reverence. Sensory input from nature generates such strong feelings of reverence that we bring the outdoors indoors at home and in our churches insofar as is possible. We make the sign of the cross with blessed water; may place a smooth, cool stone on our altar; light candles scented with pine, lemons, lilacs, and strawberries; burn sage as incense; and feel delight touching a rosary's cool wooden beads with our fingers. Indoor church decorations often include flowers, trees, bushes, pinecones, berries, stones, and rocks to name but a few.

Reverence, which comes from a Latin word meaning "awe" and "respect," refers to a deep yet exalted awareness of the Divine that allows the ego to let go (at least temporarily) of its achievement mentality so as to bring about transcendence. Great works of art, say Michelangelo's *Pietà*, may move the soul to a state of reverence resembling what mystics feel in an epiphany. Such extreme beauty commonly initiates self-forgetfulness, and the experience is so wonderful that whether it is fleeting or prolonged is, spiritually speaking, irrelevant.

The mystical poet Hafiz, who was a Muslim, expresses a value found in every religion when he writes: "I try to show reverence in all things." Fortunately, the sweeping spiritual renaissance of recent years rediscovered reverence, which was hovering near oblivion during the last four centuries of scientific dominance. For the last thirty years of the twentieth century, the renaissance has been reawakening the West to the dignity and integrity inherent in a reverent attitude toward life despite the grim media bombardment we receive day by day about terrorism, worldwide racism, genocides, and formidable degrees of corporate corruption and political malfeasance. Individuals engaged in an ongoing spiritual practice feel compassion while preventing media toxicities from getting inside their souls.

Full-blown awareness of the ecological catastrophe threatening the planet has helped revive the human passion for creation, for the sacredness and transporting aspects of nature's miraculous greening power. In the background of the Way of Light is an interplay of the highly symbolic "elements"—earth, air, fire, and water—that were cherished in the Middle Ages when people believed that these four elements were the basic building blocks of creation and vehicles for the Divine.

Just as earth, air, fire, and water constituted the essential elements of the macrocosm (the cosmos), so were they seen to function in the microcosm (the human being). The first, "earth," was thought to compose the body, as it did the planets. The second, "air," circulated in the respiratory system like the winds blowing in the cosmos. "Fire" was burning in the body, regulating temperature, even as fire was believed to burn in the sun, moon, and stars. Last, "water" moistened and streamed through the body as through the cosmos.

In the Way of Light, these four elements stand for nature in its unharmed purity and are charged with symbolic meaning. As they set the stage for each station, they heighten our awareness not only of the mysterious interplay of energies in the body and in the universe, but, more important, of the mysteries surrounding the post-Easter work of Christ. Take the Sea of Tiberias in the Tenth Station, where Jesus works a miracle: The sea is a place where much is hidden beneath the surface, and here something humanly unfathomable is transpiring. Symbolically speaking, Christ is transforming fishers into "fishers of men and women" for divine purposes.

Throughout the Way of Light, nature echoes and magnifies what is taking place among the risen Lord and his friends. Some stations are set on mountains, the traditional place where earth and heaven meet. Others take place in a garden, suggesting the seed of divinity in the soul and our creative fertility in the light of God's providential care.

In a similar vein, images of air-in-motion connote the activity of the spirit, which "blows where it will," as when Jesus breathes over his disciples in Station 7, or when rushing winds roar in the background of Station 14, Pentecost.

· REVERENCE AS SIN-PREVENTION ·

In her groundbreaking book on the labyrinth as a way of prayer, Dr. Lauren Artress discusses the role of reverence as sin-prevention. In essence, she says that when the mind is conscious of sacredness, there is no desire to engage in wrong behavior. The Way of Light does not speak of sin and does not in any way contribute to guilt trips, but one of its gifts is to awaken dormant desires for resurrection, for being reborn as a larger person. Men and women appear on the Way of Light who do remarkable, compassionate, moving things that make us aware of our own spiritual potential. It is like thinking, "If she can do that, so can I!" "If he can do that, so can I!"

I am reluctant to associate the world of "sin" with the Via Lucis, since sin prevailed so sadistically and thoroughly on the Via Crucis, wrongdoing exists, whether or not we call it sin. Humankind is naturally ego-centered, and we make more than innocent mistakes. Saint Paul mined a religious jewel and spoke for all of us in the Book of Romans when he talked about wanting to do certain things and then not doing them, while doing other things he did not want to do. Here is Paul: "Instead of doing the good things that I want to do, I carry out the sinful things I do not want to do" (Romans 7:19). Coming from a very great soul, this humble acknowledgment of sharing humankind's shadow-tendencies is very powerful. He, like all of us, makes good decisions and bad decisions, good choices and bad choices. He, like ourselves, knows the difference between right and wrong, and yet engages in wrong behavior as well as right behavior. That is the human condition.

Today we are aware of the harmful consequences of guilt trips on one hand and the need to restore a sense of sin and responsibility on the other in order to counter the unprecedented violence raging at all levels of life, in children as well as adults. Saint Paul's remark of Romans 7:19 has echoed through the centuries for a good reason: It is an excellent reminder that it is possible to balance recognition of the reality of sin with the human need to avoid excesses of guilt and shame. It is helpful to make a distinction between neurotic guilt, which is always unhealthy and excessive, out of proportion with the act committed, and normal guilt, which accurately expresses how we feel when we do something wrong. Normal guilt is healthy because it helps motivate us not to repeat a behavior, which contributes to restoring peace in the soul. By way of contrast, cold inner states aroused by neurotic guilt block our vision of God, ruin our happiness, and make love impossible. (Healing from this kind of guilt normally requires the guidance of a skilled pastoral counselor.)

One of the Greek words for sin in the New Testament is *hamartia*, which means "missing the mark," or "falling short," as in archery when the arrow goes wild and misses the target. Maybe the archer let go of the arrow a little too soon, without taking enough time to still the mind thoroughly and concentrate—like ourselves in the spiritual life. Maybe a little more mindfulness would help us reach the center, just as spiritual concentration helps us keep our sight on a distant goal that is simultaneously the center. The East sees this type of wrong or shortcoming as a failure of awareness, a kind of temporary ignorance (ignoring), and unconsciousness of how to behave rightly. The antidote is, the East believes, remaining awake.

What else can be done to avoid sin other than staying awake and being watchful? One of the most positive methods returns us to the topic of reverence, to pursuing experiences of reverence and cultivating an attitude of reverence toward everything created by God. It is impossible to be close to God and at the same time do something wrong, because the awareness of the sacred negates any desire to do something hurtful or unwise. We always have the choice of using our energy in a positive or negative way, for good or bad purposes, but when the heart is resting in joyful contentment, we are not "doing," we are not rushing, not caught in disorienting stress. Taking time to cultivate a reverent attitude through prayer and other spiritual practices, through contemplation of the ocean or a beautiful work of art, sitting in silence for five minutes to connect with the beauty of the soul, revivifies appreciation for creation.

A spiritual life that nurtures reverence for the sacred, the sacredness of the soul, the earth, the beings of the earth, and the cosmos, seen and unseen, is a way to respond to the problem of sin creatively, positively, effectively, with a lighter heart and no unnecessary guilt trips.

· PRAYER ·

Prayer is one of the most energizing, motivating, empowering, comforting, and healing forces in life. After four hundred years of scientific belittlement, its real effectiveness is beginning to be grasped again, as in the Middle Ages. Sometimes it is the pray-er who feels the results of prayer, and sometimes it is the person prayed for, as in the case of a young Marine serving in combat. When he sought help from his unit's chaplain to cope with the fear and anguish at the horror of seeing people killed every day, he paused to remark that from time to time he felt a surprising, all-pervasive sense of peace that made no sense in light of his situation. "Could it be," the chaplain asked him, "that someone at home is praying for you?"

"Yes! Of course!" came the immediate answer. "My mother."

Our realization of the power of prayer has always been based on faith that if prayer was not answered right away, it would be eventually; and if not in the way we wanted, in a way that would someday be clear. And if one were unable to pray, the Holy Spirit that illumined humankind on Pentecost would pray for us. Believing in prayer was like lighting the candle of your own spirituality; it released inner warmth and inspired compassion. Today the relationship between faith and prayer is the same, with the huge difference being that scientifically inclined researchers have put prayer to the test and have made fascinating, if as yet anecdotal, discoveries.

Tests on the effectiveness of prayer have been conducted extensively in many arenas. For example, prayer groups of devout, anonymous Christians were selected to pray at length for the healing of people hospitalized for identical serious illnesses or surgeries. In each experiment, one patient is prayed for while another is not, with the fascinating result that the person prayed for heals more rapidly and is discharged from the hospital sooner than the one not prayed for. Other experiments have shown that it does not matter if pray-ers surround a patient's bed or remain at a distance. It has also been shown that people who pray after a trauma may heal more quickly than those who do not pray.

Many studies have had similar findings, but the studies have not been done on a large enough scale, and prayer is too intangible to have produced anything but anecdotal evidence so far. But experimentation is ongoing. People with resurrection-faith have of course no need of scientific verification to evaluate the power of prayer, since we have experienced miraculous effects, but scientific confirmation of the energy that a pray-er transmits to a pray-ee might help confirm for others what they cannot yet believe. Until technology devises ways to measure this energy, let us call it "love."

Prayer adds vast dimensions of healing and meaning to daily events in the same way that grace-before-dinner transforms an ordinary meal into a gift of God, or faith turns a chance meeting into an event that was meant to be. Saint Paul counseled early Christians to "pray constantly" (1 Thessalonians 5:17), and we have been debating his meaning ever since due to the impossibility of literally "praying always." There is no better way to begin "praying always" than with a few minutes in the morning, as spending even that small amount of time may generate a little extra sensitivity, friendliness, empathy, or higher values such as mercy and forgiveness as the day goes on. This is the essential reason we pray the Way of Light: The more we pray it, the more we grow.

Prayer transforms individuals, and individuals transform the world.

· STAYING POWER ·

The spirit of exercise that lures us to the gym or the pool or the track or the dance floor mirrors the invitation to spirituality that comes from the Source of Life. It is no coincidence that words like training, practice, exercise, discipline, and health appear in both the physical workout and spiritual contexts. The flood of endorphins that can reward working out is comparable on the physical level to the flood of grace that spiritual practice can release in the soul.

A French religious order called the Little Brothers of Jesus (Les petits frères de Jesus) requires an aspirant to spend a year of novitiate alone in a hut in the desert with little but a Bible for companionship and no distractions except for occasional deliveries of food and water. When a brother who managed to survive the grueling year makes a delivery, he serves as a reminder to the aspirant that people are capable of sustaining immense hardship and passing extreme endurance tests. Those who decide to leave before the year is over learn that most of us are not called to such a radical lifestyle, but they come away with an experience of the great spiritual value to be gained from any amount of time spent in solitude and silence when the intention is higher awareness, purification of toxicities from the body and mind, and increased tolerance for difficulties.

The brothers who complete the long desert novitiate are the Western equivalent of Tibetan monks who train to become long-distance runners and eventually can cover hundreds of miles at a time. Their coaches teach them to "aim for Alpha Centauri [a remote star] and keep your eyes on your feet," which parallels the advice given to the brothers and is also the secret to living spiritually for all of us: Stay in the moment while keeping your eyes on the vision ahead.

The Little Brothers of Jesus aim at strengthening the soul while the Buddhist long-distance run focuses on the body, but spiritually speaking, the two journeys are one and the same. Regardless of the method, a person who undergoes rigorous endurance training becomes stronger. We become stronger when we undergo the much more modest training of the Way of Light. Any spiritual discipline regularly observed eases the demands of daily life and makes it possible to accomplish day-to-day tasks with an eye on the goal ahead and peace of mind in the present. That is an unconditional promise of habitual spiritual practice over time.

· THE COURAGE TO BE YOURSELF ·

A deeply moving diary written eighteen hundred years ago recounts the last weeks in the life of a twenty-year-old woman named Perpetua (ca. 182–ca. 202), who was a leader in her Christian community and a "conscientious objector" on the grounds of faith. *Perpetua's Diary* is a monument to human integrity and the courage born of conviction, and her story is unusually poignant because she was a new mother nursing her baby when she took her stand.

She was arrested for refusing to offer the annual sacrifice to the pagan gods that was demanded of every Roman citizen. When authorities offered her a second chance to make the sacrifice, she replied that she would rather die than betray her beliefs by honoring gods she could not believe in. She was imprisoned with her baby to await a hearing that would decide her fate and while there wrote her intense and vivid journal, which reveals rapidly maturing self-knowledge, self-confidence, and trust in God.

Almost overwhelmed by fear and the monumental forces working against her, Perpetua prayed for a dream of guidance and then had a series of potent, numinous dreams that gave her the courage to be true to herself. Even with her father begging her on his knees to make the sacrifice to the gods and save her life, she remained firm in her decision. The story recalls that of the Protestant reformer Martin Luther when he, at the risk of death, spoke historic words:

Here I stand.
I can not do otherwise.
So help me God.
Amen.

Some thirteen hundred years before Luther, Perpetua, too, spoke historic words when she took her final stand:

I can not
be other
than who I am.

Her story reaches extremes of courage that few of us in wealthy nations are called to emulate, but the example of remaining true to oneself under pressure has validity throughout the ages for everyone. Perpetua used every aspect of her spiritual practice not only to endure her crisis but to grow through it. She turned to God for guidance, prayed, pondered the meaning of her dreams, journaled, and discussed her plight with soul-friends from her spiritual community. Her example holds relevance for us today as a reminder that intensive spiritual work inevitably opens vast stores of grace to help us do whatever it is we need to do.

The court sentenced Perpetua to combat with wild animals in the arena. There, when she was knocked down, she slowly sat up, calmly brushed dirt off her skirt, then with perfect mindfulness reached over and picked up a hairpin she had lost and carefully replaced it in her hair. Shortly thereafter, with her dignity restored and her spirit composed, she stood up to face what lay ahead.

· HELPING THE EGO LET GO ·

Learning to let go, which is one of the primary reasons for undertaking a spiritual practice (if not "the" essential reason), is the key to being a whole person, the free self we already are but may be keeping hidden. It is like removing a tight belt at the end of a long day and feeling that we can breathe again. The body relaxes and normal spaciousness pours back into our soul from the cramped hiding places inside ourselves where we keep it compressed.

Spirituality works by enabling us to take a step back from the ego's narrow vantage point to look at things from a broader perspective. When our viewpoint opens, we see other people's attitudes more clearly and see issues in a brighter light. Problems, conflicts, and suppressed cargo from our past lose intensity and feel lighter when looked at from the wider vantage point. The decisions we make from here are more free. Greater wisdom informs our choices. When the ego is not dominating the psyche, it is the nature of the self to love, to relate without judging or being critical of ourselves or others, to stop comparing other people's "outsides" to our "insides." Many issues healed in psychotherapy resolve themselves through spiritual practice in less time and without cost.

We can prepare for letting go without straining or going to war with ourselves just by being aware that if something comes up on the Way of Light that we would like to let go of, we are willing. Once awareness is there, much of the work is done. Each time we arrive at a new station or return to it, the first practice, Relaxation and Centering, has a calming and opening effect that nurtures the process of ego-transcendence and soul-building. The qualities that we all want to see in ourselves—love, peace, wisdom, and trust—do in fact emerge in the spiritual life.

This does not mean that no effort is involved in allowing the ego to let go, as though we were opening our hands to let a butterfly fly away. Rather, the Way of Light recommends what the East calls "effortless efforting," a paradoxical approach to spiritual surrender that is active, yet free of activity; a matter of doing without overdoing, and of both being and becoming. Patience is essential on the journey.

· JOYFUL OPTIMISM ABOUT THE FUTURE: LOOKING FORWARD TO ELDERHOOD ·

A priceless gift of the Way of Light is awareness that the joy of life can continue throughout elderhood, and we can look forward to the future optimistically. When life expectancy was sixty-five, no curriculum existed for later decades, and few people could imagine a fulfilling lifestyle in their seventies and eighties. But today there is a growing realization that spirituality and service, more than anything else, make these decades joyful, active, and meaningful.

Take the example of a pianist who retired over twenty years ago at the age of sixty-five and embraced a new and original lifestyle that channeled a lifetime of learning and spirituality into useful work. Her new work consisted of a unique kind of self-giving that friends called her "spirituality of availability." Fittingly for a natural introvert who always loved to listen, she centered the last decades of her life on being there for others who needed someone to talk to, to listen to their adventures and stories and give input about problems and difficulties. Friends and three generations of family members sought her out on a regular basis, and she was always available, if not immediately, before long. She gave advice only when someone asked for it, and then it usually took the form of a story with a helpful point. Despite this altruistic "second career," this woman retained her own social life, but the thread that gave her life meaning was the decision to be available. Not surprisingly, this decidedly modern person was revered like a medieval anchorite by those of us blessed to know her.

A beautiful life like this makes many points about the healthy way to approach old age. First, this wise woman knew that elders need to feel useful, so she designed a clever new "career" in which she could minister to others' needs, yet meet her own. Second, she recognized the waning decades of life as the perfect time to do spiritual work since the psyche is freer of disquieting drives and desires than in youth or midlife: With gradually less energy available for extroverted physical pursuits, hunger for the inner life is likely to spring up of its own accord. In the spirit of the Tenth Station, where Jesus tells Peter, "Feed my sheep," this elder (who was my aunt) satisfied her spiritual hunger by nourishing others.

If physical health diminishes, the spirit of health can remain intact, as in the case of a ninety-five-year-old man of faith and prayer who was asked which decade was his favorite. Disregarding numerous physical limitations, he replied that he had enjoyed every decade but perhaps the seventies were the best. Notably, a form of body-prayer imported from China, tai chi, had helped him keep his contemplative nature alive throughout elderhood.

There is no reason to allow aging or ordinary physical infirmities to interfere with the soul's vibrancy or the spirit's relationship with God. Among the blessings gained from prayer is increased spiritual strength for dealing with illness, physical loss, and feelings of vulnerability that may accompany sickness. In addition to showing that others praying for ill people may assist healing, as was mentioned above, researchers have observed that when the ill person also prays, recovery proceeds more rapidly.

· A VISION OF THE BEST ·

The higher values of mercy, forgiveness, compassion, responsibility, and sacrificial love are returning to civilization after a long absence. They remain mostly invisible at the level of politics and business, but spiritual values are incarnated in individuals, not the collective. Saints, sages, and mystics who carry these values across time have reentered our awareness and passed them to us through CDs, books, tapes, and other media. As we re-inherit the timeless Christian legacy from these great souls, we relearn the truth about human life and in addition discover in their example a spiritual attainment that we all secretly long for.

Mother Teresa never tired of saying that "Everything begins with prayer," which is the key to a vision of life at its best, one brimming over with blessings and the "joy that is full and more than full." Love, faith, hope, purpose, and devotion, to name only a few, characterize the life of prayer and should be envisioned as real possibilities on the path, at every age. The cure to every problem in the world lies ultimately in loving children and giving them a positive, empowering vision of the future at its best. In the absence of love and hope, youthful depression and despair reach epic proportions and ruin young lives. Opportunities for nurturing and inspiring children and adolescents have never been more obvious than today nor more within the reach of almost everyone.

One of the first benefits of spirituality is recognizing God's initiative in our lives. God is constantly reaching out to us through apparently ordinary events and the people who come and go in our lives on an average day. Spiritual vision sees that plain daily occurrences are revelatory of the divine and can be woven into our destiny like golden threads. Everything has a reason and destination. Nothing happens by chance. Spiritual practice changes us, and part of the transformation is a vision of life at its brightest and most beautiful.

HOW TO PRACTICE THE
WAY OF LIGHT

One day you finally knew
what you had to do, and began.
MARY OLIVER

Today millions of poor children raised in big cities never get to see the stars, as bright city lights block out the nighttime sky. This inestimable deprivation, like the world's ecological loss, parallels our personal diminishment when we do not have a daily spiritual practice. The writer Thomas Berry made a wonderful remark in this context: "What happens to the outer world happens to the inner world. If the outer world is diminished in its grandeur then the emotional, imaginative, intellectual, and spiritual life of the human is diminished or extinguished."

Spiritual practice accomplishes what nothing else in life can, the miracle of awakening to a new vision of yourself and imagining a new way of being in the world. From this broader and happier perspective, you may be surprised to find how wide your heart can open, how tenderly you can express yourself, and how deeply caring you can be when responding to the needs and hurts of others. But this is precisely what can happen when you practice the Way of Light.

This chapter contains a brief explanation of the ten spiritual exercises that you will practice at each station in Part II, which is the devotional section of the book. At the end of the chapter you will find a set of additional practices that you can use from time to time. For example, if one of the basic practices does not appeal to you, you could substitute one of these supplemental exercises for the unsuitable one. It is important to remember that no exercise is ever required. You will gain the most spiritual benefit from doing the exercises that fit your temperament and personality.

Here are the practices for praying the Via Lucis:

Practice 1: Relaxation and Centering
Practice 2: Reading the Story
Practice 3: Imagining Yourself in the Story
Practice 4: Meditation
Practice 5: Journal Reflection
Practice 6: Insights and Illuminations
Practice 7: Releasing Your Creativity
Practice 8: Prayer for Today
Practice 9: Asking for a Spiritual Gift
Practice 10: Giving Back to the Community

· PRACTICE 1:
RELAXATION AND CENTERING ·

Christian mystics have taught throughout the ages that "nothing is as close to God as silence." The "Relaxation and Centering" exercise begins the process of drawing you into silence and through silence into oneness with the infinite love in the soul and the universe. This exercise borrows some of the most beautiful methods in Eastern religions such as Buddhism and Hinduism and combines them with tried and tested techniques from the Christian mystical tradition to help you learn to still your mind and directly encounter the God of love.

The practice takes a different form at each station so you learn a total of fourteen varying methods for entering silence. They all entail concentration to focus your energies and empty your mind of distracting thoughts that interfere with the experience of stillness. As you learn to focus your attention, you become increasingly aware of the richness and fullness of God's presence in the quiet mind.

While the primary intention of the "Relaxation and Centering" exercise is to be with God, you may experience a number of other outcomes. You will surely observe yourself deepening spiritually, or as Meister Eckhart would say, "sinking" into deeper spaces in your soul where your relationship with the divine becomes increasingly transformative. Meister Eckhart advised, "Sink eternally," signaling the virtual limitlessness of this path to deepening and to knowing God.

Also, because breathing techniques from the East are woven into this exercise, you may see benefits from this part of the practice appearing spontaneously during stressful occurrences day by day. Not only does breathing properly calm nervousness and build your power of concentration, but scientific studies have also demonstrated remarkable benefits to health and well-being from meditative breathing practices. Among them are lowered blood pressure and respiration, deeper brain waves, slower cardiac rhythms, and decreases in hormonal levels associated with stress.

Other elements of this practice may remind you of the tradition of Centering Prayer, which dates back to the desert fathers and mothers of the fourth century and was revitalized in the 1970s by Trappist monks. At one of the stations the practice invites you, as does Centering Prayer, to choose a sacred word (a mantra) to repeat prayerfully when your mind strays in order to restore your focus (other benefits of mantra praying are discussed below).

Here are the subjects of the "Relaxation and Centering" practice:

Station 1: Entering Silence, p. 89
Station 2: Finding Spaciousness, p. 98
Station 3: Repeating "I Love You," p. 107
Station 4: Invoking God's Presence, p. 116
Station 5: Moving toward Stillness, p. 125
Station 6: Picturing a Beloved, p. 133
Station 7: Breathing in Peace, Breathing Out Stress, p. 141
Station 8: Emptying the Mind, p. 149

· PRACTICE 2: READING THE STORY ·

The Way of Light honors fourteen stories from the soul-making and community-building days of the original Easter season. Like all good stories, these invite you into a world where you can see in a new way. Symbolic words and pictures tell universal truths that you can find echoing in your own experience. Stories awaken the inner intuitive nature that the din of home entertainment media dulls in much of the world today. Here, sadly, the art of storytelling as an oral form no longer captivates listeners of all ages in every village with compelling tales that rush toward emotional excitement, then to calmness and back again. But the art form perseveres in scattered indigenous cultures around the world that remain close to the earth and are too poor to have electricity.

Native American storytellers who were once central to tribal identity and continuity through the generations appear to be vanishing. But native artists have immortalized the enchantment through charming sculptures, wood carvings, and paintings of a fantasized storyteller with a flock of children in her arms who are entranced by the wonder in her tale. Hopefully the future will preserve these artistic monuments of an ancient way of life alongside books and CDs of sacred teachings about the Great Spirit and the interconnectedness of all beings on earth.

The Way of Light stories, which are two thousand years old, come from the generation of people who knew Jesus personally, including his mother and siblings, friends, the twelve apostles, and other women and men who traveled with him. As their generation died out, the stories were transmitted orally and also written down by many people, often in the form of a letter from the leader of a community to his congregation. Letters from four such leaders, Matthew, Mark, Luke, and John, which were gathered into the New Testament (along with Paul's and others'), are the sources of the stories in the Via Lucis. Laboriously copied and recopied by hand in beautiful, often illustrated manuscripts, the stories have been painstakingly preserved through the centuries, and as of the invention of the printing press in the sixteenth century, printed Bibles allowed for their worldwide dissemination for the first time. The Bible is the best-selling book of all time.

· PRACTICE 3:
IMAGINING YOURSELF IN THE STORY ·

This practice, which has been adapted for this book from the famous "spiritual exercises" of Saint Ignatius Loyola, is a form of sensual-imaginative prayer. The method guides you to imagine yourself as an eye-witness to the original story by using all of your senses—seeing, hearing, touching, tasting, and smelling—to re-create the scene. After that, you imaginatively enter into relationships with the persons in the story to share their unparalleled experience of Resurrection faith.

By bringing together the pleasure of the senses with the creative imagination, the exercise allows you to become a character in the story with your own thoughts, feelings, opinions, and conscience. Feelings cover a broad spectrum from painful loss to ecstatic joy, and you may find yourself raising questions you never thought of before and reflecting on mysteries from an attitude of faith.

The practice begins by picturing vividly whatever details your imagination presents to your senses. You may see the natural beauty of mountains or the sea; taste fresh-baked bread, delicious fruits and nuts, or homemade wines; you may touch natural textures like homespun wool;

hear the sounds of the city and the countryside; feel the sensuality of the spring; or watch clouds and birds come and go. What you imagine is a virtually limitless expression of your own individuality.

The next part of the practice helps you connect to people in the story, as though you were there with them in the passion of the moment, sharing the excitement, concern, frustration—whatever the story presents for imaginative amplification. If you allow your ego to let go and give your imagination free rein, Jesus, Mary his mother, Mary Magdalene, Peter, the Emmaus disciples, and anonymous poor and well-to-do followers will become real as never before. You will overhear conversations and join in, feeling with the protagonists, understanding them more deeply, finding how contagious their wisdom is, and seeing how they symbolize the human condition and real-life situations we face today.

· PRACTICE 4: MEDITATION ·

In contrast to the stillness and passivity of the mind required in Eastern meditation and in Christian contemplative prayer, the meditation form used in this book calls for the mind to be actively engaged in thought and reflection. It is more like Teresa of Avila's "mental prayer" than like the Eastern forms of meditation so widely practiced in the West today.

Buddhist monks and Hindu spiritual teachers have contributed invaluably to the West's renewed interest in contemplative prayer by teaching a generation of restless Christians to sit still and concentrate. They have reminded us that in silence it is possible to experience oneness with God. While the East prefers words like "emptiness" or "ultimate reality" to designate the goal of spiritual attainment rather than the word "God," the experience is the same. When an American monk who has practiced contemplative prayer for twenty years in a church meets a Buddhist monk who has meditated for twenty years in a cave, they describe the same beauty, wisdom, dreams, and ordeals.

In this book, Eastern religions have influenced the design of the "Relaxation and Centering" practice (see above) but not the Meditation practice. Considering this, it is recommended that you read the meditation very slowly, pausing as often as you wish to think about the ideas and allow your feelings, memories, and insights to surface for reflection. Optional questions at the end of each meditation guide you to interrelate with the contents of the meditation in the interest of evoking your individual spiritual possibilities, simply and comfortably. There is no "right answer" anywhere in this book; only suggestions to help you open the inner doorway to a wisdom that will remain with you on the best days of your life and the most difficult. Here are the topics of the meditations:

Station 1: The Buried Seed Bursts Open and Rises to Life, p. 91
Station 2: The Spirit Works Through Surprises, p. 101
Station 3: A New Kind of Love Relationship, p. 110
Station 4: Mary Magdalene's Calling Is Our Calling, p. 119
Station 5: Strengthening the Soul for the Journey, p. 127
Station 6: Breaking Bread Together, p. 135
Station 7: "Divine Psychotherapy," p. 144
Station 8: The Power of Forgiveness, p. 151
Station 9: Seeing What Is Hidden, p. 161
Station 10: Sacred Love, p. 169
 Loving Unconditionally, p. 170
Station 11: Sacred Authority, p. 179
Station 12: Between Two Worlds, p. 187
Station 13: Waiting for an Explosion of Wisdom, p. 195
Station 14: Being a Way of Light, p. 203

· PRACTICE 5: JOURNAL REFLECTION ·

A notepad and pen or pencil suffice for the Fifth Practice, and a computer or laptop is fine, too, if that is what you prefer. But most people like to keep a special journal that they enjoy looking at and holding in their hands, perhaps as a respectful reminder of the content's sacredness. The purpose of the journal exercise is to increase self-knowledge, which, as Saint Augustine wrote in his *Confessions,* is the truest way to knowledge of God.

You may wish to utilize the journal for reflection on other matters during the days you are practicing the Way of Light, especially if you are using the fourteen-week schedule, praying one station each week. On this extended schedule there is lots of material to choose from, such as surprising events and conversations as well as dreams, which are always a source of the unexpected. It is helpful to respond in writing to the question that C. G. Jung, who wrote widely on the religious unconscious, recommended raising after each dream: "What is the purpose of this dream?" What is it trying to teach you? What do you need to learn at this time?

The same questions can be posed, of course, after other life events. During the time you are working with the Way of Light, it is likely that your answers to Jung's question will be connected to the powerful archetypes associated with the station. So you may wish to process, to think about, the occurrence in relationship to the station you are currently working with. You might respond to a question like this one: "What have I learned from the Via Lucis that can help me understand this situation (or event, person, problem, hurt, and so on)?" Or if you need to make a decision, you could look to the Way of Light for guidance, but it is always best to devise your own approach.

Keeping a journal provides a lasting record of spiritual growth, one that is more accurate than memory. Rereading the journal to review the course of your pilgrimage greatly enhances awareness of what happened, prevents denial, helps with resistance, and is there for future review. It should be treasured as part of your spiritual autobiography.

Here are the subjects of journal reflections:

Station 1: Awakening, p. 93
Station 2: Surprised by Joy, p. 102
Station 3: Turning and Re-turning to God, p. 112
Station 4: Seven Blessings, p. 120
Station 5: Knowing Your Inner Strengths, p. 129
Station 6: Feasting, p. 137

· PRACTICE 6:
INSIGHTS AND ILLUMINATIONS ·

This exercise consists of a number of inspirational passages from Christian and non-Christian spiritual leaders, poets, and scriptures to enrich your practice and for you to enjoy whenever you need spiritual nourishment. The content, which suggests the station's principal theme without adhering to it rigidly, is intended to elicit feeling and intuition, humankind's most spiritual gifts. Other practices are more conducive to thinking, like the "Journal Reflection," while still others highlight imagining, as in Practice 3. But it is important to note that, despite emphases, each practice addresses the whole person: spirit, mind, and body.

There are many pathways of devotion, and usually we choose the one that best fits our personality and temperament. Some people prefer to think about the deep things of the Spirit, others like to feel and intuit the Spirit's presence, while others connect to God through the sensual beauty of nature. The practices in *The Christian Way of the Light* seek to be inclusive of different personality types and preferences. Certain practices may appeal to you less or more than others, but it is wise to do all of them to have an experience of your whole being in the presence of God.

· PRACTICE 7:
RELEASING YOUR CREATIVITY ·

This exceptionally important practice celebrates humankind's capacity to create, which is the source of our uniqueness as a species on earth and the closest we come to being like God in the original act of Creation (Genesis 1:1–2:4a). Other species function by instinct, rote, programming, or varying cause-effect sequences. The human species uniquely creates. What you create is a prayer, a sacred way of consciously participating in the holiness of life and connecting with the Source of Life.

The spirituality of creativity lies additionally in the power of the creative process to awaken or reawaken dormant spirituality. The artist in each of us can come alive through the simplest act of making something original, in part because of the self-forgetfulness implicit in the process. Engaging in the work of making, of creating, is sacred because the ego lets go of its desires and a larger self performs the work in imitation of God. There is no better way to awaken creativity than through spiritual practice.

Another aspect of the spirituality of creativity lies in the meaning, direction, and fulfillment that a creative project gives the maker at each stage of bringing something new into existence. Like the drama of the little seed germinating underground that suddenly bursts into light, grows, and blossoms into a flower, a creative project serves as a way for the creative spirit to enter life and work marvels. Each stage of the creative process is a gift of grace and a source of grace. From the initial, elating ah-ha experience that gives birth to a new image, the idea for the project, through the exciting stage of planning, then the laborious execution phase, to the final completion of something that has never been before: Cooperating with grace, you are a cocreator with God, as St. Hildegard said.

The quality, relative value, beauty, or merit of the object that you create is irrelevant. Being yourself and making something out of your soul's inner core is what counts, whether a delicious meal for a loved one, a sculpture, collage, or cure for a disease. All created objects have equal spiritual worth. The value has to do with honoring your soul's favorite method of creative expression and then taking the leap into the life of the creative spirit to give birth to something new, something that has never existed in quite this way until now. There is no need to be a professional artist, dancer, writer, or anything else to birth newness: All of us can.

Here are the topics of the creativity practices in *The Stations of the Light*:

Station 1: Creating Inspirational Post-its, p. 95
Station 2: Drawing, Dancing, or Singing Your Prayer, p. 104
Station 3: Creating a Mantra (Sacred Word), p. 113
Station 4: Soul-gardening, p. 122
Station 5: Mapping Your Journey, p. 131
Station 6: Seeing God in the Breaking of Bread, p. 139
Station 7: Bringing Beauty into the Day, p. 147
Station 8: Creating a Forgiveness Process, p. 155
Station 9: What Is Your Image for God? p. 164
Station 10: Drawing a Mandala, p. 173
Station 11: Finding a Simple Way to Serve, p. 182
Station 12: Dialoguing with a Prayer, p. 191
Station 13: Creating a "Mary Prayer," p. 199
Station 14: Writing a Psalm of Praise, p. 207

Be sure to save writings, drawings, collages, songs, or other creative products that result from your practice of the Way of Light, so you may look back at them and review your growth as you proceed from station to station. You may notice, say if you choose to draw or paint, the colors and shadings that attracted you at the time. What does that say about "where you were at," spiritually speaking, when you did that drawing or painting? Does that work indicate, say, one of the four seasons?

If you write, pay attention to themes and images that appear to see what you can learn from them. Gather together all these created products that result from praying the Way of Light repeatedly over the course of time, and you will have a book of symbols that belong to your spiritual autobiography, as they illustrate the unfolding of your inner life while practicing this devotion and reveal the evolution in the way you envision God.

· PRACTICE 8: PRAYER FOR TODAY ·

Each station includes a well-known Christian prayer or prayerlike sacred poem that expresses a central spiritual message of the station. The prayer exercise, like all practices for the Way of Light, is meant to evoke the spiritual potential of the whole person and foster intimacy with God.

Although the ancient custom of memorizing virtually died out with the advent of the Information Age and easy online research, some people like to memorize the kinds of prayers found in this book. Elders learn them by heart to fight memory loss, and younger men and women memorize prayers (as well as the Insights and Illuminations of Practice 6) to have comforting, reassuring, or inspiring words available in times of stress, boredom, waiting, or discomfort.

The act of remembering words that you love has many rewards. It offers all the benefits of focusing the mind, such as letting go of fears and environmental chaos, to achieve an experience of peace. It puts time to gracious use, and, as some prayers calm while others excite energies, it is helpful to have prayerful words in mind to meet the demands of the moment. Helping small children memorize prayers has beneficial effects on the whole family.

Here are the fourteen prayers used in this book. Be sure to substitute or add your own if you wish:

Station 1: While Learning to Sing, p. 96
Station 2: "Troparion," p. 105
Station 3: God Showed Me in My Palm, p. 114
Station 4: "Go Now, My Friend," p. 123
Station 5: I Have Always Known, p. 131
Station 6: "Our Father," p. 139

· PRACTICE 9: ASKING FOR A SPIRITUAL GIFT ·

As each Station of Light draws toward a close, Practice 9 offers you an opportunity to experience and appreciate the power of spiritual intention by asking for a spiritual gift. Intention is not like a petition for something concrete that you want, the way a child prays, but is more like giving your consent to God's action within. Then your spiritual possibilities reach new dimensions. Just by entering willingly into a trusting relationship with God, you are opening to the blessing you seek, and there is no end to the grace available for growth.

When you do Exercise 9, you may intuitively know what gift would best serve your spirituality. Is it a question of quenching a spiritual thirst or of support or strengthening that you need in some area? Is it motivation to do something you "ought" to do, or courage to let go of the "ought" and search for guidance? Do you need to ask for more compassion toward yourself or others? Or to be freed of an inner burden such as racism or classism? If you are not sure what to ask for, consider questions like those and look back over your responses to the first eight practices to see what comes up. Or think about the gifts of the Holy Spirit mentioned by the prophet Isaiah: wisdom, insight, counsel, power, the spirit of knowledge, awe before God (Isaiah 11:2), and, as the New Testament adds, devotion.

The gift may arrive disguised, requiring reflection and interpretation, and it may come in a series of small packages. Watching for spiritual connections over the course of a day does not guarantee an abundance of moving encounters on that day, but it does promise increased awareness of the spiritual abundance in daily life and the ability to see more than you would without conscious intention. Or to take another example, perhaps you are looking for mastery over a tendency you dislike in yourself. Placing this desire in the realm of intention while giving consent to divine activity is to bring it into the dimension of grace where a struggle with self-mastery may soon melt into an act of letting go.

If you are the kind of Christian who prefers giving to receiving, it is important to remember that Practice 9 is for yourself, not for friends, family, or the world. This is the only exercise that counsels you to ask for something for yourself. The last exercise, Practice 10, returns to the giving mode.

· PRACTICE 1O: GIVING BACK TO THE COMMUNITY ·

The closing practice invites you to give back to the community in gratitude for all the blessings you have received, especially the gift of life itself. The spirituality of gratitude has two parts: the first pertains to awareness of grateful feelings and expressing them, and the second is about finding concrete ways to give back.

It is not difficult to be grateful when we are happy. Most people who see a little animal run out from under a bush feel a burst of excitement that is like a prayer of praise. But wisdom teachers are always reminding us to be grateful for "everything," meaning the difficulties and hurts as well as the joys and rewards. As Saint Paul puts it: "Give thanks in *all* circumstances," not just in pleasant ones. In very difficult times, managing to express gratitude is an acknowledgment of faith in God and yourself, like saying that you know you can get through it, no matter how hard it is.

The mystical poet Christopher Smart—who called the Psalms "the Great Book of Gratitude"—wrote a masterpiece of praise and gratitude,

Jubilate Agno, when he was confined to debtors' prison, sick and miserable. The poem is an ecstatic outpouring, page after page, of lists of things for which he is grateful, such as Geoffrey, his cat, "the servant of the living God" who "purrs in thankfulness"; and for nutmeg and lightning; also the letters of the alphabet, because they are the beginning of learning; colors, too, because they are spiritual; sunshine that illumines the air with brightness; the man on the corner who loaned him money; and the blessing of God on grass in shades of green; plus dozens more.

It is especially powerful to engage in the prayer of thankfulness at dusk, the traditional time when monks and nuns pray Vespers, when an atmosphere of mystical wonder is hovering over the earth and the moon and stars are coming into view. This is a very good time to think about giving back. Whom could you reach out to right now? What could you do or begin doing tomorrow? Who or what cause needs you? If you can spare only a minute at this time in your life, how could you put that minute to good use?

Gallup polls show that almost 90 percent of men and women report that expressing gratitude makes them happy; perhaps the same number of people would say that giving back makes them even happier.

· ADDITIONAL PRACTICES ·

Here are a few extra practices that you may wish to substitute for those described above from time to time.

1. FINDING YOUR PRAYER

In many Native American traditions, it is customary for each person to compose a "death song," a private prayer that he or she will sing once and once only, at the moment of death. If such a beautiful practice ever existed in the Christian tradition, it has been lost. Perhaps the closest we come lies in a little-known custom of writing our own prayers to carry with us through life in a journal or a particular notebook.

The Catholic scholar John O'Donohue has improved on this exercise in his book, *Eternal Echoes,* with advice for creating a special prayer from the center of the soul, even if contriving it takes a week or months or a year. Here are his recommendations:

> Listen to the voices of longing in your soul. Listen to your hungers. Give attention to the unexpected that lives around the rim of your life. Listen to your memory and to the onrush of your future, to the voices of those near you, and those you have lost. Out of all that, make a prayer that is big enough for your wild soul, yet tender enough for your shy and awkward vulnerability; that has enough healing to gain the ointment of divine forgiveness for your wounds; enough truth and vigor to challenge your blindness and complacency; enough graciousness and vision to mirror your immortal beauty. Write a prayer that is worthy of the destiny to which you have been called.

2. MINDFULNESS

All of the practices in this book aim at nurturing mindfulness, or awareness of what is happening in the present moment without projecting into the past or future. Thinking excessively about the past can lead to getting lost in old hurts, while too much thought about the future can result in projecting troubles that never arise. Mindfulness training, which came to the West from Eastern religions in the waning decades of the twentieth century, consists of spiritual practices to awaken consciousness of the inner life and alertness to surroundings in the here and now.

A world-famous mindfulness teacher with extraordinary soul-beauty and a rare degree of attainment, Thich Nhat Hanh is a Vietnamese Buddhist monk, the author of *Being Peace* and many other beautiful books. He is a living embodiment of mindfulness (as well as many other spiritual teachings). At the World Parliament of Religions in 1993, conference participants returning from lavish meals in Chicago's posh restaurants were shocked to find Nhat Hanh and two brother monks sitting in a small circle, cross-legged, on a sidewalk. There, with the deafening noise of people yelling at one another, honking horns, screeching brakes, and hundreds of people brushing by, they were silently and very slowly eating vegetables from small paper bags. The monks ate in perfect concentration, as though they were at home in a monastery.

Here is one of Thich Nhat Hanh's mindfulness practices as taught by one of his students; it is a lesson in the bliss of taking forty-five minutes to eat an orange:

Plan a time and place free of interruptions, and begin by holding the orange in your hand, contemplating it for a long time. Carefully observe every detail that your five senses present for your consideration. Enjoy contemplating the roundness of the orange, its aroma and vivid color. Feel the cool skin, how it feels in the hand and to the fingers. Turn it round and round to savor the weight and shape in your hand, taking note of marks or color changes on the skin. Notice the delightful feelings that come up. When you are ready, peel a tiny piece of skin very slowly. Look at the orange flesh and how it shines as though a bright light were inside. Smell the inimitable fragrance. Eventually taste a single drop of the delicious juice. Continue cherishing every sensation that the orange can provide until the last bite is swallowed three quarters of an hour later.

If two or more people perform the practice together, it is best to do so in silence. You will enjoy the experience of inter-being, a phrase that Thich Nhat Hanh coined to convey the profound interconnectedness that joins all beings to one another.

An unusual story about the concentration that can result from mindfulness training concerns a corporate CEO who was sitting at his desk talking on the telephone when there was a sudden loud roar followed by a violent crash and the sound of shattering glass. Office personnel came running and found the businessman quietly continuing the phone conversation as though oblivious to what had happened: Melting ice and snow two feet thick had slid off the roof of the next building and come crashing through the huge window behind the CEO, dumping piles of snow on the floor and splintering glass all over his desk, shoulders, and hair. Only when he had finished the conversation and hung up the phone graciously did he permit himself to react to the intrusion. Then his hands shook and his face turned white.

3. CREATING A MANDALA

The word mandala, which comes from the Sanskrit word for circle, refers to a sacred design enclosed within a circle. Mandalas have been objects of meditation in the East for millennia. As the round shape implies a center, mandala-meditation is seen as a pathway to the center of consciousness. The word is also a compound composed of *manda,* meaning "essence," and *la,* meaning "container," so a mandala is considered to "contain essence," and meditating on a mandala is a way to experience oneness with essence or, in Christian language, union with God. Some spiritual seekers draw a mandala on a regular basis to unlock their souls.

Few people in the West were aware of these abstract, often intricate forms before the twentieth century, when C. G. Jung, the founder of analytic psychology, began observing them in his patients' dreams and studying their origin in Eastern religions. Jung found mandalas preponderant in the Buddhism of Tibet, where the art was refined in monasteries over the course of thirteen hundred years for purposes of meditation. Since the Chinese occupation of Tibet in the 1950s, Tibetans in exile have shared the sacred art and practice with the world.

In one Buddhist tradition, nuns work painstakingly for five days to construct a six-foot-wide mandala from multicolored sand. At the end of the week, a beautiful sand painting covers a long table. Almost as soon as the work is finished, flutes, bells, and drums signal the beginning of a sacred ritual that concludes with the destruction of the mandala to signify the impermanence of material things. Onlookers may be given a teaspoon of the sacred sand in a small envelope.

In the United States, the delicate multicolored sand paintings made by Navajo Indians exemplify this art form. Like their Buddhist counterparts, they often destroy the sand paintings upon completion as a reminder of impermanence.

Similar rituals exist in Latin America and all over the world. In Latin America, on certain festivals, flowers are used to create a beautifully designed carpet that will cover an entire street closed off to traffic. At the end of the festival, a crowd walks down the street, ruining it. In India's Kashmir Sivaism, to give an example, a sand mandala may be delicately crafted on the ground at the doorway to the ashram, where devotees will eventually ruin it by walking through it to enter the building, implying that renunciation of materialism opens a doorway to the divine.

4. KIND THOUGHTS

Developed by Fr. Lawrence Lovasik, the "practice of kind thoughts" is a lovely, thoughtful approach to relationships based on the principle of seeing others as they appear to another person, also to someone who loves them, and to God. He provides questions to think about from each person's perspective when an issue, situation, or conflict needs to be resolved.

Instead of reserving the "practice of kind thoughts" until there are difficulties, however, it is best to begin using it when meeting another person for the first time. Father Lovasik advises reflecting on the Creator's infinite love for the soul in order to become mindful of God's particular love for each and every individual.

Father Lovasik's healthy and loving model recommends healing conflicts before they spiral out of control. It is central to take the other person's feelings into consideration as soon as possible after conflict erupts by, first, placing yourself in that person's position and, second, asking yourself questions about how the situation appears to the other person. For example: How would I be judging the issue if I were "in their shoes"? What would I be wishing for if I were that person? What would I wish to say or do?

Imagining yourself in the place of someone who loves the other person is also advocated. Father Lovasik recommends looking at the situation as, say, the person's mother would, and considering the same questions from her point of view. How might a loving mother (or whatever person you decide to imagine here) judge the issue? What would she be wishing for? What would she wish to say or do?

Another aspect of the exercise suggests placing God in the situation with the people involved. This time the questions to think about relate to God's viewpoint. How might God regard the situation? What does God desire for each of these individuals? What would God wish to say to them or do for them?

5. ADORATION

The custom of kneeling before the Blessed Sacrament for an hour of contemplative prayer, which was popular in monasteries and lay religious movements from the Middle Ages to the Second Vatican Council (1962–65), is being revived in the United States and abroad today. The movement to renew the ancient devotion of Perpetual Adoration is spreading among growing numbers of laypeople hungry for tranquillity and closeness to God.

Adoration chapels connected to Roman Catholic parish churches are beginning to dot the American landscape, remaining open twenty-four hours a day seven days a week so that men and women, regardless of their work schedules, can spend an hour in deep prayer.

A fairly typical adoration chapel is the one attached to St. Patrick's Church in Natick, Massachusetts, which is flourishing under the inspiring leadership of Fr. Brian Kiely. It is never empty. Parishioners sign up well in advance for an hour of contemplation, and at every hour of the day or night, at least one person and usually many more will be found kneeling or sitting before the Blessed Sacrament in silent prayer.

Entering an adoration chapel is like walking into the Holy of Holies in an ancient temple. The room is not a place to escape from the world's chaos and violence but rather an island in the middle of the storm where you can be with God for a while in deep silence. The beautiful and loving atmosphere in an adoration chapel makes it an ideal place for praying the Stations of the Light.

6. SACRED GESTURES

Two sacred gestures found throughout the world that you may wish to incorporate into your practice of the Way of Light are kneeling and bowing. As an alternative to sitting or standing during prayer, kneeling is highly conducive to good concentration, centeredness, and a healthy flow of energies of the body. In the kneeling posture, the full length of the spine is kept as straight as possible, which facilitates breathing from the diaphragm rather than from the chest. (If you happen to be familiar with the Eastern chakra system, the advantages of kneeling will be obvious.)

If you decide to kneel for a part of the Way of Light, practice will show you what is the right length of time for you. Some people are comfortable kneeling for an hour or more, which would cause others physical discomfort. Five to twenty minutes works well for a number of people, while others do not wish to kneel at all. Practitioners of Eastern religions sit still with legs tightly crossed in the yoga style for hours, but few Westerners adapt well to that posture. It is generally advisable for Americans to avoid stress from uncomfortable postures that might distract attention from the purposes of the devotion and even lead to the abandonment of the practice.

Another ancient and very beautiful tradition that you might like to include with the Way of Light is the custom of bowing, which has been a feature of Christian liturgies throughout the centuries but antedates Christianity by thousands of years. For many practitioners in the East, an especially reverent devotion calls for repeating the bow literally dozens of times. One Eastern method that is highly visible in the West today consists of lowering oneself slowly to a kneeling position on the floor and bending forward until the forehead gently touches the floor. The hands are placed palms down on the floor on either side of the head. Due to the widespread dissemination of Eastern ideas and practices in the West today, it is not uncommon to see individuals bow like this in a Catholic adoration chapel.

Another version of bowing requires standing with the hands clasped together in the prayer position at the center of the chest, then bowing forward slightly from the waist as in the familiar Japanese way of greeting, a gesture of respect and honor for the person bowed to. This bow is also part of the ritual of the Mass. You may wish to try genuflecting, kneeling on one knee and returning right away to an upright posture, as before entering a church pew.

Another variation consists of kneeling on the floor and bending forward slightly with the hands joined in the classical prayer position at the center of the chest.

Bowing can be a devout and energizing supplement to the Way of Light. Either the standing or kneeling bow could be repeated, say, three times at the beginning and/or close of each practice when it is natural for energy to shift and thoughts to distract attention. If the practice appeals to you, allow yourself to be as creative as possible intermingling bowing with the Way of Light.

7. THE JESUS PRAYER

The habit of saying the "Jesus Prayer" appeared in the earliest centuries after Christ and is one of the most powerful devotions in the Christian tradition for stilling an agitated mind and a disturbed body. But the prayer has far greater benefits than calmness, some of which are described with immense beauty in *The Way of a Pilgrim*, one of the world's religious masterpieces, written by an anonymous Orthodox monk and published in Russia in 1881. Pilgrim monks reciting the Jesus Prayer were seen wandering the Russian countryside from the Middle Ages until the Revolution of 1917.

In the following passage, the author quotes instructions for saying the Jesus Prayer that he found in the *Philokalia* (meaning "the love of the beautiful"), which was published in Greek in 1782 and remains one of the most beautiful books in the literature of prayer. An Eastern Orthodox anthology containing eleven hundred years of writings on prayer, the *Philokalia* belongs to the tradition of hesychasm, meaning quietness or silence. The passage quoted in *The Way of a Pilgrim* comes from Saint Symeon the New Theologian (949–1022). Here it is:

> Find a quiet place to sit alone and in silence, bow your head and shut your eyes. Breathe softly; look with your mind into your heart; recollect your mind—that is, all its thoughts—and bring them down from your mind into your heart. As you breathe, repeat: "Lord Jesus Christ, have mercy on me," whether quietly with your lips, or only in your mind. Make an effort to banish all thoughts; be calm and patient, and repeat this exercise frequently.

Various forms of the prayer have emerged over the centuries. One is, "Jesus, son of David, have mercy." Another version is "Jesus son of David have mercy on me." Some people pray "Lord Jesus, son of God, have mercy," while others alter it to "Lord Jesus Christ, have mercy on me." You may wish to shorten the prayer to "Jesus son of David," or to create your own variant of the prayer. You need to decide also whether you want to say the prayer out loud, silently, or in a whisper. At a more advanced stage of practice, the prayer will say itself without prompting and without interrupting what you are doing.

The author of *The Way of a Pilgrim* describes joy while reciting the Jesus Prayer; you may have had a similar experience enjoying nature:

> [E]verything around me seemed delightful and marvelous. The trees, the birds, the earth, the air, the light . . . seemed to be telling me that they witnessed to the love of God for humankind, that everything proved God's love for humankind, that all things sang a prayer of praise to God. . . . the prayer of my heart gave me such comfort that I felt there was no happier person on earth than I and I doubted that even in heaven there could be any greater and fuller happiness.

8. PRAYING WITH A MANTRA

A mantra is a sacred word or phrase that is repeated or chanted over and over to free the mind of thoughts and open the mind, heart, and body to

God. It is not uncommon for a Hindu spiritual teacher to counsel a re-treatant to sit under a tree for two hours continually repeating a personal mantra. In certain parts of India where people recognize 108 names for God, spiritual aspirants may repeat their mantra 108 times anywhere from several times a day to weekly or less often. You may wish to choose a number that holds symbolic meaning for you.

It is likely that Hindu sages were chanting mantras on the banks of the Ganges five thousand years ago. The custom of sacred repetition made its way into Christianity with the practice of the "desert" fathers and mothers in the early centuries of church history. The renewal of the custom in our times is due largely to the influence of Eastern religions.

There are at least four types of mantras from which you can choose or, preferably, you will create your own. The first type is a simple prayerful word, such as "God," "Lord," or "Love," or you may opt for a word from a foreign language, perhaps "Ram," an Indian name for God, or "om," which Hinduism sees as the ultimate sound in the universe, the most sacred sound. Early Christians employed an Aramaic word that makes an excellent mantra, *maranatha*, meaning, "Come, Lord Jesus."

A second approach is to borrow a favorite brief verse from the Gospels, say Jesus' affirmation to the disciples, "I am always with you" (Matthew 28:20b); or the angel's reassurance to Mary Magdalene, "Do not be afraid" (Matthew 28:5a). Also, Peter's response to the risen Lord when he questioned Peter's love: "Lord, you know I love you" (John 21:15b), or merely, "I love you." All three of these and many others belong to the Way of Light.

Spiritual affirmations are a third type of mantra, such as "I breathe in peace" (or love, forgiveness, freedom, joy, and so on). Also "I love," or "I am loved," plus innumerable others can be used.

A fourth type encompasses brief petitionary prayers for a spiritual need to be met at the present time. Among these are "Help me, Lord," or "God, give me wisdom (or strength, faith, grace, patience, courage, peace, and so on). Another mantra of this type, "Center my heart in yours, O Lord," emerged from the Centering Prayer movement founded by the Trappist monks at Saint Joseph's Abbey in Spencer, Massachusetts: Fathers Basil Pennington, Thomas Keating, and William Meninger. The Jesus Prayer fits with this category of mantra.

· CREATING MARY MANTRAS ·

In light of the global renaissance of devotion to Mary the Mother of Jesus, it is surprising that no "Mary Prayer" paralleling the Jesus Prayer has come along. Recent years have brought about the revitalization and expansion of the Rosary; worldwide honoring of the Black Madonna and new shrines to her; and extensive apparitions of Mary in Europe and the Americas, and yet it appears that there are apparently no new "Mary mantras." An equivalent of the Jesus Prayer could be "Mary, mother of us all, have mercy." It is moving and would raise awareness of the sacred feminine. Mary mantras would serve the same purpose, in addition to all the other calming and liberating effects of sacred repetition.

A vast treasury of ancient litanies to Mary, prayers, hymns, and thousands of lines of exquisite poetry, exist from which to fashion mantras. For instance, "Mary, mother of the Lord, be with me." Or "Mary, star of the sea, watch over us." "Mary, queen of heaven, pray for us." "Mary, mother of us all, give me strength" (or any other spiritual gift that you need in the moment).

It is best to pray your mantra as often as you can, walking, climbing stairs, cooking, and when anger or another potentially harmful emotion comes up. As Eastern Orthodox monks wrote in the *Philokalia*, "Take up a word of love, and stay quietly with God." If you go to bed reciting your mantra, you may find yourself waking up in the morning saying it, an auspicious way to start the day.

· · ·

Just as your body needs regular exercise and physical nourishment to remain healthy, your spirit needs spiritual practice and nourishment to awaken and be strong. The practices that follow in Part II of *The Christian Way of Light* were created and arranged in an intentional way to nurture you for the journey and bring out your spiritual potential while you journey from chapter to chapter—and in an ongoing way. Saint Teresa of Ávila wrote that "in the spiritual life we are either going for-

ward or we are going backward." If she were alive today, she would probably insert times of plateau, of rest, between the extremes, but her
concern about the human tendency to self-sabotage would remain un-
changed. Discernment is necessary to recognize the difference between
"rest" and "resistance." And needless to say, Saint Teresa would call you
back to prayer the minute she saw resistance setting in. For prayer is the
one certain way to go forward knowing God, loving, and seeing the
world in all its sacred radiance.

· SCHEDULES FOR PRACTICING THE WAY OF LIGHT ·

A FOURTEEN-DAY JOURNEY

The Stations of the Light lend themselves perfectly to a two-week retreat
that you can make in your own home. You will need to set aside an hour
each day for fourteen days, preferably in the morning, so that its beautiful
energy will nourish you as you go through the day.

If you wish to divide your practice of the Way of Light into half an
hour mornings and evenings, it is recommended that you follow the order
of the exercises given in the book, performing the first half of the exercises,
numbers 1 through 5, as the day begins, and the latter ones, 6 through 10,
in the evening.

A THREE-DAY RETREAT

If you would like to practice the Way of Light on a retreat, there are several approaches. You might make a private retreat at a spiritual center you
are familiar with where a sister, priest, or lay spiritual director could serve
as a guide, or you could remain at home and serve as your own director.

There is too much material to cover in three days, so you will need to decide how many practices you believe you can comfortably complete over the course of a day. One approach is to omit all Optional Practices and do only the Recommended Practices, which follow here:

Recommended Practices

Practice 2: Reading the Story
Practice 3: Imagining Yourself in the Story
Practice 4: Meditation
Practice 5: Journal Reflection

The Recommended Practices require about a half hour. You will need to schedule five stations (1 through 5) for the first day, five stations for the second day (6 through 10), and four (11 through 14) for the last day. Here is a typical schedule:

Friday

9:00–9:05 a.m.	Relaxation and Centering Practice, p. 58
9:05–9:30 a.m.	Station 1
11:00–11:30 a.m.	Station 2
1:00–1:30 p.m.	Station 3
3:00–3:30 p.m.	Station 4
5:00–5:30 p.m.	Station 5

Saturday

9:00–9:30 a.m.	Station 6
11:00–11:30 a.m.	Station 7
1:00–1:30 p.m.	Station 8
3:00–3:30 p.m.	Station 9
5:00–5:30 p.m.	Station 10

Sunday

9:00–9:30 a.m.	Station 11
11:00–11:30 a.m.	Station 12
1:00–1:30 p.m.	Station 13
3:00–3:30 p.m.	Station 14
3:30–3:35 p.m.	Asking for a Spiritual Gift, p. 69
	Giving Back to the Community, p. 70

It is wise to keep the schedule open and flexible, adapting it to your own changing needs.

A FOURTEEN-WEEK RETREAT

Another approach to the Via Lucis consists of practicing one station a week for fourteen weeks. Hopefully with this longer method you will have time to finish all ten practices, which takes about an hour. It is especially important to select a place, day, and time that you can adhere to for the duration. It is best to plan a fourteen-week retreat when it will not be interrupted by a vacation or major holidays. But if you need to interrupt the schedule, return to the spiritual practice as soon as possible at your usual place and time.

WITH A SMALL GROUP
OR CHURCH COMMUNITY

Another model for any of the retreat forms described above suggests praying the Way of Light with a small group, say no more than sixteen people, which is the limit for preserving openness and intimacy. The advantage of group work relates to enriched friendships, fresh ideas and insights, increased compassion, and plans for further spiritual work together. Additionally, group members often discover an immediate opportunity to serve within the group.

If you have persuaded your parish to build a set of Stations of the Light in the church, garden, or adoration chapel, then your group can walk the Via Lucis together. Instead of following the recommended practices, the group should preselect the exercises for each station, depending on the amount of time you have, and choose a leader to give instructions. Here are suggestions for group practice of each exercise, although you will probably do no more than five practices at each station:

> Practice 1: *Relaxation and Centering.* A volunteer reads the instructions very slowly while the group does the exercise.
>
> Practice 2: *Reading the Story.* Ask for a volunteer to read the story for the station being practiced.
>
> Practice 3: *Imagining Yourself in the Story.* Each person does the exercise silently, then the group shares results (without obligation to participate).
>
> Practice 4: *Meditation.* Read the meditation and answer the questions silently, then share answers, insights, or reflections with the group (no obligation to participate).
>
> Practice 5: *Journal Reflection.* Group members journal silently. Then, depending on the time available, a number of volunteers share with the group.
>
> Practice 6: *Insights and Illuminations.* Proceeding clockwise around the group circle, each person reads one out loud.
>
> Practice 7: *Prayer for Today.* A volunteer reads it to the group.
>
> Practice 8: *Creating Inspirational Post-its.* Each person journals a favorite thought from the practices of the day to post in a prominent place at home, enter into a computer file, or memorize. Then everyone shares with the group.
>
> Practice 9: *Asking for a Spiritual Gift.* Individuals write in their journals what gift they are requesting, then those who wish share with the group.
>
> Practice 10: *Giving Back to the Community.* Everyone journals on different ways of giving back in gratitude, then those who wish share with the group.

WITH A PRAYER PARTNER

Praying the Way of Light with a like-minded person is like visiting a wonderful museum with a friend: The beauty of the experience is doubled. And when the topic is spirituality, there is the added dimension of invaluable feedback that trusted friends can give one another.

The instructions given above for a group also apply to prayer partners. Before beginning, you might like to read a helpful book such as the classic *Soul Friend* by Kenneth Leech or the ancient treatise on spiritual friendship by the Cistercian mystic Aelred of Rievaulx.

WHEN YOU HAVE ONLY FIVE MINUTES

When you cannot take the time for a retreat, try spending five minutes doing any one of the exercises for any station. Doing this can give you the spiritual gift needed in the moment.

Part II

• • •

PRACTICES

JESUS RISES
FROM THE DEAD

He is not here; for he has risen, as he said he would.
MATTHEW 28:6A

Practice 1

RELAXATION AND CENTERING:
ENTERING SILENCE

Begin Practice 1 by sitting in a comfortable, upright position, hands resting in your lap, eyes closed, feet flat on the floor. Allow your spine to be as straight as possible without tightening any muscles.

Bring your attention to your breathing. Feel the breath ebbing and flowing in your body. Does it appear to be located in the chest? Or in the nostrils? Or abdomen? Or somewhere else? Notice the quiet rise and fall of the in-breath and the out-breath, allowing yourself to become more and more still with each breath. Take a moment to rest in the peacefulness.

When you are ready, focus your attention on the pause between breaths. It may be very brief and barely discernible, or it may seem long to you. In the space of this fleeting pause where one breath dies and another rises, is silence. In this nearly imperceptible space, you touch God.

The more you practice this exercise, the less elusive is the sacred interval. Continue to focus gently on the space between breaths for a few minutes. Do not hold your breath. If you find your mind wandering, gently bring it back to the sacred space between the in-breath and the out-breath knowing that you are entering more and more fully into the silence of God.

As your practice of the Way of Light advances and deepens, you may wish to spend considerably more time with this exercise.

Practice 2

◆

READING THE FIRST STORY

The angel said to the women, "There is no need for you to be afraid.
I know that you are looking for Jesus, who was crucified. He is
not here; for he has risen, as he said he would.
Come and see the place where he lay."
MATTHEW 28:5–6

Practice 3

◆

IMAGINING YOURSELF
IN THE STORY

To pray with your whole self—body, soul, and mind—allow your senses to come to life through the following practice, entering personally into the sacred event as though it were taking place right now and you were there.

It is Sunday morning just before dawn, and Jesus' closest women disciples—Mary Magdalene, Mary of Bethany, Joanna, Salome, and Mary the mother of James—arrive at the sepulchre where he was placed on Friday. In your imagination place yourself with them, holding a torch in one hand and in the other an alabaster bowl of sweet spices to anoint the body. Now, holding your torch in the doorway, look inside the tomb. Can you see the table where the body was placed? What else do you see? Do you hear anything? How large is the space? Are the walls whitewashed or made of earth or stone or something else? What is it like for you to look into the tomb and see that the body of your beloved Teacher is not there? What do you feel? What are you thinking?

Now imagine an angel appearing and telling you that Jesus has risen from the dead. How do you respond to this staggering turn of events? You look at the other women. How are they reacting?

Now the angel invites you to enter the tomb. Do you hesitate before following him? What are you thinking? Inside, in the torchlight, you notice that the white linen cloths in which Jesus' body was wrapped on Friday and the napkinlike cloth that you yourself placed on his face are still there, undisturbed, unmoved, as though he had slipped away right through them. Go over and pick up the napkin. What is it like for you to touch those sacred cloths? Do you feel moved to pray? To kneel? To hold out your arms in wonder? Speak your prayer now.

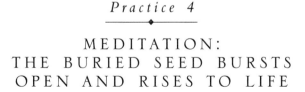

Practice 4

MEDITATION: THE BURIED SEED BURSTS OPEN AND RISES TO LIFE

The world-transforming story you read today is set in the first light of dawn by an empty tomb with a wide-open entranceway where the earth itself is pulsating with growing life energies. Unseen seeds are bursting with sacredness. Invisible sprouts are shooting up to fill the world with beauty and a light brighter than the sun, moon, and stars. An angel appears, like the angel who came to tell Mary the mother of Jesus that she would birth a savior, and once again humankind receives a message of amazement, of love, of transformed destiny and infinite mystery.

This miraculous setting, like a birthing room or a womb that is erupting with new life and possibility, is the very opposite of a place of death, loss, grief, and finality. It is a place of rebirth, renewal, revival, and recovery, a space more sacred than anywhere else on earth this first Easter morning. Wondrous and awesome, mind-baffling and soul-shattering, it is a tomb, but it is an empty tomb, marvelously empty, yet with an earthen floor like our souls. And this dawn, this sacred dawn, has followed the darkest of all possible dark nights.

Women who loved Jesus with all their hearts arrive with burning torches so that in the dim firelight, they can see. They anticipate impenetrable darkness but instead are nearly blinded by the arrival of a celestial being blazing with light that makes the dark tomb radiant. He counsels the awestruck women that there is no reason to be afraid. And then without further preparation he delivers mind-bursting news. Jesus is risen. He is alive. Go quickly, he adds, and give his disciples this message: "He has risen from the dead and now he is going before you to Galilee; it is there you will see him" (Matthew 28:7b).

The message is meant not only for the inner circle, the original disciples, but also for their successors, ourselves. The risen Lord goes before us, too, on our own journeys. And we who died and rose with him in our baptism can stand at the doorway to the empty tomb in blazing light, fully awakened, fully aware of the truth and beauty in his timeless words:

I tell you most solemnly,
unless a grain of wheat falls on the ground and dies,
it remains only a single grain;
but if it dies,
it yields a rich harvest.

JOHN 12:24

• *Thinking about your real possibilities and limits, how can you be more like the person you wish to be?*

• *What in you needs to come out of the tomb of darkness into light? An attitude, feeling, belief, problem, or something else?*

• *We have a physical relationship with the world and a mystical relationship with the world that enables us to see God everywhere. Where, in what kinds of situations, do you see the presence of God?*

Practice 5

◆

JOURNAL REFLECTION: AWAKENING

The pattern of our lives follows the rhythm of the paschal mystery, of dying and being reborn. Awakening follows sleep, and spiritual awakening needs to occur when we fall spiritually asleep. In your journal, reflect on one or more of the following questions:

• *Where do you see God at work in your life, bringing newness out of something that is coming to an end?*

• *Where do you see God at work in the world, bringing new life out of something that is coming to an end?*

• *Does this help you to trust the Christian teaching that, no matter how grave the future of the planet may appear, grace triumphs in the end?*

Practice 6

◆

INSIGHTS AND ILLUMINATIONS

and how could anyone believe
that anything in this world
is only what it appears to be—

MARY OLIVER

I found the world wrapped in an inexpressible glory with its waves of joy
and beauty bursting and breaking on all sides. The thick cloud of sorrow
that lay on my heart in many folds was pierced through and through by the
light of the world, which was everywhere radiant. . . . There was nothing
and no one whom I did not love at that moment.

RABINDRANATH TAGORE

Love is the person of the resurrection scooping up the dust and
chanting, Live.

EMILY DICKINSON

There is no whole heart but a broken heart.

ANONYMOUS CHASIDIC MASTER

We live now no longer for ourselves alone, but we live hidden with Christ.

COLOSSIANS 3:3

When you walk down the street, an angel of the Lord goes before you
calling out, "Make way. Make way for the image of God."

EASTERN WISDOM

This is what we proclaim to you:
  What was from the beginning,
  what we have heard,

what we have seen with our eyes,
what we have looked upon
and our hands have touched—
we speak of the word of life.

I JOHN I:I

Then thought I to understand this,
but I could not
until I went into the temple of God.

PSALM 73:16–17

The world and time and all created by God are eastering and rising up to
life again. The universe and all of us are the result of unbearable tenderness,
and we are laced and threaded with everlasting life that cannot and will not
ever be undone. Hope surrounds and delight stalks our every step, because
Love still reigns and seeks us out no matter where we hide or live.

MEGAN MCKENNA

Practice 7

——◆——

RELEASING YOUR CREATIVITY: CREATING INSPIRATIONAL POST-ITS

If you wish to do this exercise, you will need a package of Post-its and a
pen or pencil. Copy onto a Post-it a sentence, passage, or verse from one
of the practices for Station 1 that is especially moving or meaningful to
you. Post it in an area where you will see it frequently, say on the inside
of a closet door, on the refrigerator, or on a bulletin board so you can
reread the message often for inspiration. You may like to memorize se-
lections so you can think about them when you are away from home.
This practice is particularly helpful to elders who want to prevent mem-

ory decline. (For more about the Practice of Sacred Post-its, see my book, *Sacred Voices*.)

Practice 8

—————◆—————

PRAYER FOR TODAY

There is a brokenness
out of which comes the unbroken,
a shatteredness out
of which blooms the unshatterable.

There is a sorrow
beyond all grief which leads to joy
and a fragility
out of whose depths emerges strength.

There is a hollow space
too vast for words
through which we pass with each loss,
out of whose darkness
we are sanctioned into being.

There is a cry deeper than all sound
whose serrated edges cut the heart
as we break open
to the place inside which is unbreakable
and whole,
while learning to sing.

RASHANI, CONTEMPORARY HERMIT

Practice 9

———◆———

ASKING FOR A SPIRITUAL GIFT

In the light of the following passage from Jesus' teachings, what spiritual gift or blessing would you like to receive today?

Ask, and it will be given to you;
search, and you will find;
knock, and the door will be opened to you.
For the one who asks always receives;
the one who searches always finds;
the one who knocks will always have the door opened to him.

MATTHEW 7:7–8

Practice 10

———◆———

GIVING BACK
TO THE COMMUNITY

Think of a simple way to "give back" to life today as an expression of gratitude for all the blessings you receive.

WOMEN FIND
THE EMPTY TOMB

The angel said to the women,
"There is no need for you to be afraid."
MATTHEW 28:5A

Practice 1

RELAXATION AND CENTERING:
FINDING SPACIOUSNESS

Begin your practice today by sitting in a comfortable, upright position, hands resting in your lap, eyes closed, feet flat on the floor. Allow your spine to be as straight as possible without tightening any muscles.

This exercise combines Eastern and Western meditation methods to help you become aware of yourself as spirit. Gently close your eyes and begin imagining that your body is hollow. See that there is nothing inside you but space. And there is nothing outside you but space on all sides. All that separates the inner space from the outer space is a light veil of skin.

Now notice your breathing. Breathe normally and naturally. As you inhale, imagine the pores of your skin opening and allowing more space to pass into your body. As you exhale, allow the breath to pass out through the same pores. Repeat several times. The in-breath brings spaciousness in through the skin, and the out-breath lets it go out through the skin.

Become aware that you are in a vast universe of pure space, empty of all material things, filled with the invisible presence of Pure Spirit. Feel yourself as spirit. Know how close you are to God's Spirit. Continue breathing spaciousness in and out through the pores of the skin. Remain quietly here in this sacred spaciousness for a minute or two.

Practice 2

READING THE SECOND STORY

*After the Sabbath, and toward dawn on the first day of the week,
Mary Magdalene and the other Mary went to visit the sepulchre.
And all at once there was a violent earthquake; for an angel of the
Lord, descending from heaven, came and rolled back the stone and
sat on it. His face was like lightning, and his robe white as snow. The
guards were so shaken, so frightened of him, that they were like dead
men. But the angel spoke, and he said to the women, "There is no
need for you to be afraid. I know you are looking for Jesus, who was
crucified. He is not here; for he is risen, as he said he would."*
MATTHEW 28:1–6A

Practice 3

———◆———

IMAGINING YOURSELF
IN THE STORY

To pray with your whole self—body, soul, and mind—allow your senses to come to life through the following practice, entering personally into the sacred event as though it were taking place right now and you were there.

Imagine that you are standing before the sepulchre with Mary Magdalene and the other women, staring at the immense stone blocking the entranceway to the tomb, wondering how it can be moved. Just then an angel appears right in front of you. How do you react? Are you terrified? Do you feel an urge to run away? Or is it wondrous and awe-inspiring? Look carefully at the angel. He is blindingly beautiful, dressed in radiant clothes like white light. What is the effect on you? Notice the guards. They cover their eyes to hide from the sight and are totally frozen in fear.

Suddenly you hear a deafening roar like an earthquake. You watch totally transfixed as the angel reveals the full majesty and might of angelic power by rolling away the huge stone as though it were made of paper. Now you see with your own eyes that the tomb is empty! What is that like for you? What are you thinking? What are you feeling?

You look at Mary Magdalene, a woman of deep prayer and wisdom. What does she do? Does she cry out? Watch her body language. Is she more able to cope with this shock than you? Or is she shaken to her core, her mind spinning with frantic questions about who took him away or if he might still be alive in some safe place? What are you thinking? Listen as the angel begins to speak. His very first words are: "There is no need for you to be afraid." Does that help you to center and be still? Now he delivers the great news that Jesus has risen from the dead. What is this like for you? What is it like for Mary Magdalene? In your imagination, go over and speak to her. What do you say? What does she say in response?

Practice 4

———◆———

MEDITATION: THE SPIRIT WORKS THROUGH SURPRISES

Read the following words very slowly, pausing as often as you wish to reflect.

Women come to the empty tomb and are shocked by a sudden earthquake, a trembling of the earth as though the earth's crust were rupturing from unstoppable movements underground. It is like the rupture of childbirth or the parting of the sea at the exodus, a symbol of massive divine intervention in the life of humankind. A monumental breakthrough of love has shattered the entire course of the world, raising the crucified God from the dead, bringing him back to his loved ones so that they—and we—can live in the light.

As the earthquake roars and rips at the earth's sacred ground, disciples in fear and trembling, shaken to their core by the sheer magnitude of the surprise, encounter another unexpected event. An angel manifests. But an angel is a place of refuge, a presence of goodness and help, and he calms and comforts them through a few simple, strengthening words: "There is no reason to be afraid." God's Spirit is at work. God's Spirit works through surprises. It is wiser to trust the mystery of the unexpected than to fear.

This teaching holds ultimate wisdom for each of us. The Spirit works through surprises in everyone's life. Every minute of the day brings the possibility of a surprise, the possibility of a breakthrough of love, of newness and change and joy. A split second can turn a day inside out. Even the seemingly smallest event, like a chance remark that we happen to hear or a butterfly that suddenly comes and goes, can open a gateway to an unknown field of blessings and abundance. And when the surprise is difficult and challenging, people of resurrection faith know that the Spirit is in this, too. And that makes all the difference. There is no reason to be afraid. We can be like the priest who prays after every event in his life, joyful or sorrowful, "This, too, art Thou."

It is wise to be wakeful, to pay close attention to feelings of being startled or afraid. An image may be coming to mind of something we can create or of someone we can help. Let us open our hearts and minds to the real possibility, the likelihood, that we will be surprised today. Let us trust that an unexpected event, a sacred moment, will be rich with precisely what we need, or a loved one needs. A healing. A teaching. An invitation. An answer to prayer or sheer bliss. Let us be watchful and wait with wide-open eyes as the day unfolds, reminding ourselves that powerful divine energies are always at work in our bodies and souls and those of everyone else, seeking to interrupt boredom and repetitive tasks, to alleviate unrelenting stress, to resolve persistent problems, to make our dreams and visions come true.

- *Try taking the time to reflect on the meaning of a surprising event.*
  What benefits can you gain by pausing to think about the meaning?
  Would it strengthen your faith?
- *The Spirit works through coincidences, which are a form of surprise.*
  What was the last coincidence you experienced? Did you look for the
  spiritual teaching in that event? What did you learn?

Practice 5

◆

JOURNAL REFLECTION: SURPRISED BY JOY

List five of the most joyful surprises of your life. Then focus on one of them, and respond in your journal to these questions:

- *Who was an instrument of the Spirit in this experience?*
- *What did you learn from that experience about the way the Spirit*
  works in our lives?

• *Who else benefited from this in-breaking of the Spirit in your life? That is, was there a ripple effect?*

Practice 6

◆

INSIGHTS AND ILLUMINATIONS

All things work together for good for those who love God and are called according to God's purpose.

ROMANS 8:28

I come in the little things,
says the Lord.

EVELYN UNDERHILL

Wherever there is an empty space, there the presence of God is found.

THE TALMUD

For the Lord your God is bringing you into a good land, a land of brooks and water, of fountains and springs, flowing forth in valleys and hills, a land of wheat and barley, of vines and fig trees and pomegranates, a land of olive trees and honey, a land in which you will eat bread without scarcity, in which you will lack nothing, a land whose stones are iron, and out of whose hills you can dig copper. And you will eat and be full, and you will bless the Lord your God for the good land he has given you.

DEUTERONOMY 8:7–10

My soul is not asleep.
It never sleeps, nor dreams,
but watches wide awake
things far away.
While listening

at the shore
of silence.
ANTONIO MACHADO

There is no need for you to be afraid.
MATTHEW 28:5

All shall be well,
and all shall be well.
All manner of thing shall be well.
JULIAN OF NORWICH

Practice 7

◆

RELEASING YOUR CREATIVITY: DRAWING, DANCING, OR SINGING YOUR PRAYER

Even if you do not think of yourself as an artist, allow your creative self to release your own unique response to the story of the empty tomb. Employ any form of artistic expression that you enjoy, say drawing, painting, sculpting, singing, dancing, writing a poem, cooking a special meal, or creatively using materials that are available in your surroundings. Please disregard your skill level. Let the artist in you bring into being something that has never existed before, and you will come as close as human beings can to the mystery of God's creation of the cosmos. There is no more sacred act.

Practice 8

◆

PRAYER FOR TODAY:
"TROPARION"

Lord,
This woman who encountered her shadow
   perceives the numinous in You,
   leads the women who come with grief
   and myrrh to Your grave.
Alas! What a desperate night I've traveled through:
   extravagant the desire, dark and moonless
   the need of a passionate body.
Accept this spring of tears,
   you who empty the seawater from the clouds.
Bend to the pain in my heart, You
   whose incarnation bent the sky
   and left it empty.
I will wash Your feet with kisses,
   dry them with my hair, feet that Eve once heard
   at dusk in Paradise, then hid in fear.
You who are limitless mercy—who will erase the results
   of a lifetime I've done wrong, evaluate
   my weakness? I ask, remember me
   if nothing else, as one who lived.
KASSIANE (TRANSLATED BY LIANA SAKELLIOU)

Practice 9

◆

ASKING FOR A SPIRITUAL GIFT

What spiritual gift or blessing would you like to receive today?

Ask, and it will be given to you;
search, and you will find;
knock, and the door will be opened to you.
For the one who asks always receives;
the one who searches always finds;
the one who knocks will always have the door opened to him.

MATTHEW 7:7–8

Practice 10

◆

GIVING BACK
TO THE COMMUNITY

Think of a simple way to "give back" to life today as an expression of gratitude for all the blessings you receive.

JESUS APPEARS TO MARY MAGDALENE

Jesus said, "Mary!" She turned and said to him in Hebrew, "Rabboni!" (which means Teacher).

JOHN 20:16

Practice 1

RELAXATION AND CENTERING: REPEATING "I LOVE YOU"

Begin your practice today by sitting in a comfortable, upright position, hands resting in your lap, eyes closed, feet flat on the floor. Allow your spine to be as straight as possible without tightening any muscles.

Gently bring your attention to your breath, becoming aware of the natural flow of the in-breath and the out-breath. If you are breathing heavily or rapidly, allow the ebb and flow to slow and become more quiet. Now imagine the in-breath flowing gently into the heart region in the center of your chest, and the out-breath flowing lovingly back into the world. With each inhalation allow divine love to fill your heart, and with each exhalation say slowly and silently: "I love you." Repeat the practice as long as you wish, for at least a minute or two. If an image of a person you love comes to mind, gently let go of it by returning your attention to God, repeating the words "I love you."

If you wish, you may simply repeat the words without paying any attention to the breath. Simply say "I love you" as slowly as you wish, letting some time elapse between repetitions.

Practice 2
◆
READING THE THIRD STORY

Mary Magdalene stood weeping outside the tomb, and as she wept she stooped to look into the tomb; and she saw two angels in white, sitting where the body of Jesus had been, one at the head and one at the feet. They said to her, "Why are you weeping?" "Because they have taken away my Lord," she replied, "and I do not know where they have laid him." As she said this, she turned around and saw Jesus standing there, but she did not recognize him. Jesus said to her, "Woman, why are you weeping? Who are you looking for?" Supposing him to be the gardener, she said, "Sir, if you have taken him away, tell me where you have put him, and I will go and remove him." Jesus said, "Mary!" She turned and said to him in Hebrew, "Rabboni!" (which means Teacher).

JOHN 20:11–16

Practice 3

◆

IMAGINING YOURSELF IN THE STORY

To pray with your whole self—body, soul, and mind—allow your senses to come to life through the following practice, entering personally into the sacred event as though it were taking place right now and you were there.

Imagine that you are sitting at dawn in the garden by the tomb where Jesus rose from the dead. Not far from you is Mary Magdalene, who is weeping over the loss of the Teacher who was the center of her life but was killed and has disappeared. Suddenly though, a radical shift in the energy occurs, as though she (and you) had awakened abruptly from a nightmare: A man whom you take to be the gardener engages Mary in a poignant, profoundly moving, and beautiful dialogue. See how your emotions parallel hers as she realizes who this gardener is. Watch what powerful feelings flow in their voice tones, facial expressions, and body language.

GARDENER: Why are you weeping? Who are you looking for?
MARY MAGDALENE: Sir, if you have taken him away, tell me where you have put him, and I will go and remove him.
JESUS: Mary!
MARY MAGDALENE (turning): Rabboni! (which means Teacher).
JESUS: Do not cling to me, for I have not yet ascended to the Father. . . .

How does Mary Magdalene look as she speaks to the "gardener"? How would you describe the tone of her voice? The expression on her face? Right after that, Jesus speaks her name. What is the tone of his voice like? What is it like for her to hear her name spoken by someone she thought was dead?

Now imagine that Jesus calls out your name in the same tone of voice. What is that like for you?

Watch as Mary slowly turns toward Jesus and in a flash of intuition suddenly recognizes him. How does she look now? What can you see in her eyes? Is it joy? Ecstasy? Or something too sacred to describe?

Continue watching as she rushes over to the risen Lord and embraces him rapturously—just as you would if a loved one who had died were to suddenly reappear. Jesus very briefly returns her embrace and then steps back, saying the world-famous words with which Titian entitled his beautiful painting, *Noli me tangere;* Do Not Cling to Me. Are you surprised? What kind of response on his part would you have preferred? Go over to Mary and say what is in your heart. How does she respond to you?

Practice 4

◆

MEDITATION: A NEW KIND OF LOVE RELATIONSHIP

In this pivotal scene from the Way of Light, Mary Magdalene is often compared to the "loving, searching woman in the *Song of Songs*" who tries to find her beloved in the darkness of night. Symbolically, both women seek the Divine Beloved. But the object of Mary Magdalene's search is also a man of flesh and blood who healed her of deep pain, gave her a purpose in life, and taught her how to be strong, spiritually and morally. Jesus awakened Mary's heart as no one had before and taught her how to trust and how to love. Since then, she has walked with him and his small group of disciples all over Palestine, listening to his amazing teachings with awe and delight, pondering their meaning until they now form part of her soul and she knows every teaching by heart. Mary understands that Jesus was speaking in parables so that listeners would have to think and raise questions and penetrate meanings for themselves, as on the day he compared the kingdom of God to a mustard seed.

Now she is in a garden by a sepulchre where disciples put his body, and he has disappeared. She is desolate, as any of us would be, completely abandoned and alone. But her despair does not last long. She hears her name called out in the semidarkness and turns toward the familiar, tender voice, her eyes filling with light. This act of turning toward the Divine Beloved brings a flash of recognition, a radical shift in her whole body, mind, and soul, like awakening from a deep sleep.

Mary runs over to Jesus to grab him and hug him and hold on to him. She wants things to be the way they were, to recover her Teacher and go on as in the old days. But he tells her not to hold on anymore, not to cling. She has to let go of the way things used to be. She has to let go of the old relationship. It is time to embrace a new way of relating that is better, since it can never end. Hard as it seems, there will be infinite joy in knowing him for the rest of her life as risen and living in her heart.

The act of turning, the simple gentle gesture of looking toward the source of the voice that calls her, transforms Mary Magdalene's attitude totally, as it does ours. Sometimes the difference is sudden and stunning, like nighttime shifting to midday, and at other times gradual, like dawn coming slowly in. But the outcome is always the same. When we turn or return to the one who is always speaking our name, a welcoming love rises in our hearts as though we had finally come home. The prophet Isaiah hears God saying personally to each of us, "I have called you by name. You are mine . . . and I love you" (Isaiah 43:1). The God of love is incapable of abandoning us. Divine love is integral to our being and can never disappear, whether we are turning away or turning back.

- *The Hebrew word that we translate as "repent" originally meant "return." Does turning to God in prayer help you repent?*
- *What else does the act of "turning" symbolize to you? Sudden growth? Turning to God when one has lost one's way? A shift of attitude from doubt or fear to faith? Recovery from depression? A religious conversion experience?*
- *Have you discovered a lasting relationship with God? Or does it still ebb and flow?*
- *Would you compare your awareness of God's presence to forgetting and remembering? If so, how can you improve your spiritual memory?*

Practice 5

◆

JOURNAL REFLECTION: TURNING AND RE-TURNING TO GOD

Turning to God is often called a "conversion experience." But conversion is a repeated process rather than a once-in-a-lifetime event. We turn to God and re-turn again to find our way after falling off the path. As Saint Augustine taught, we regularly make the mistake of "forgetting" God, and the only remedy is to "remember" God again. Describe in your journal an experience of "forgetting" God and how you turned back to God. Who helped you? What would help you to avoid "forgetting" God again?

Practice 6

◆

INSIGHTS AND ILLUMINATIONS

By night I sought Him whom my soul loves.
SONG OF SONGS 1A

My one thought is to love you.
THÉRÈSE OF LISIEUX

Forever at his door
I gave my heart and soul. My fortune, too.
I've no flock anymore,
no other work in view.
My occupation: love. It's all I do.
JOHN OF THE CROSS

As a deer longs
*   for flowing streams*
so longs my soul
*   for you, O God.*

PSALM 42:1

Many waters cannot quench love, nor can floods drown it:
if a man offered for love
all the wealth of his house,
it would be utterly scorned.

SONG OF SOLOMON 8:7

When the heart grieves for what it has lost, the soul rejoices
for what it has found.

SUFI SAYING

O my Lord,
stars glitter
and the eyes of men are closed.
Kings have locked their doors
and each lover is alone with his love.
Here I am, alone with you.

RABIA (717–801)

Practice 7

RELEASING YOUR CREATIVITY: CREATING A MANTRA (SACRED WORD)

Today's Relaxation and Centering exercise invited you to concentrate on a silent repetition of the mantra "I love you" (mantras are discussed on pp. 79–80). In your journal, create five mantras. Select the one that "feels right" to be your personal mantra (knowing you can change it later if you need to). Repeat it slowly and reverently for at least a minute, allowing the words to take root in your soul. Remember to use your mantra as a regular part of your spiritual practice.

Practice 8

———————◆———————

PRAYER FOR TODAY

God showed me in my palm
a little thing round as a ball,
the size of a hazelnut.
I looked at it with the eye of understanding
and asked myself:
"What is this thing?"
And I was answered:
"It is everything that is."
I wondered how it survived
since it seemed so little,
as though it could disintegrate in a second
into nothingness.
The answer came:
"It exists and always will exist,
because God loves it."
Just so does everything have being
because of God's love.

JULIAN OF NORWICH

Practice 9

———— ◆ ————

ASKING FOR A SPIRITUAL GIFT

What spiritual gift or blessing would you like to receive today?

Ask, and it will be given to you;
search, and you will find;
knock, and the door will be opened to you.
For the one who asks always receives;
the one who searches always finds;
the one who knocks will always have the door opened to him.

MATTHEW 7:7−8

Practice 10

———— ◆ ————

GIVING BACK
TO THE COMMUNITY

Think of a simple way to "give back" to life today as an expression of gratitude for all the blessings you receive.

MARY MAGDALENE PROCLAIMS THE RESURRECTION TO THE APOSTLES

Mary Magdalene went and said to the disciples, "I have seen the Lord."
JOHN 20:18A

Practice 1

RELAXATION AND CENTERING: INVOKING GOD'S PRESENCE

Begin your practice today by sitting in a comfortable, upright position, hands resting in your lap, eyes closed, feet flat on the floor. Allow your spine to be as straight as possible without tightening any muscles.

Gently focus your attention on your breathing for about a minute until you feel your mind becoming still and your heart-center opening. Now picture yourself sitting quietly opposite Jesus, Mary, a favorite saint, or a spiritual teacher who has brought you closer to God. Become aware of the divine love in this person who has invited you to the place where you are now. Know that this channel of love is filling your soul this very minute with grace. Blessing after blessing is being placed on your path. Breathe deeply to release any resistance in your body or mind, allowing yourself to be fully aware of the holy presence opposite you, inside you, all around. Know that this spiritual presence is always with you, and it can never be otherwise. Rest for a few minutes in the security of being with God.

Practice 2

———◆———

READING THE FOURTH STORY

Jesus said to Mary Magdalene, . . . "Go and find my brothers and tell them that I am ascending to my Father and your Father, to my God and your God." So Mary Magdalene went and said to the disciples, "I have seen the Lord"; and she told them that he had said these things to her.
JOHN 20:17B–18

Practice 3

———◆———

IMAGINING YOURSELF IN THE STORY

To pray with your whole self—body, soul, and mind—allow your senses to come to life through the following practice, entering personally into the sacred event as though it were taking place right now and you were there.

Imagine yourself in the garden where the risen Lord has just appeared in his Resurrection body for the first time, astonishing Mary Magdalene (and you). Dawn is breaking all around you. Do you see and hear the wonders taking place: birds beginning to sing, flowers opening, animals waking up, the earth alive with the vibrancy of a new day? How does this beautiful garden change with the growing light? What colors can you see now? What fragrances do you notice? Touch a few of the plants nearest you: What different textures can you feel? What sounds do you hear? Are there aromatic spices and herbs? Which ones do you recognize? Which fruit trees and nut trees do you recognize? Are they flowering, growing, or ready to harvest?

Now look at Jesus, and listen with awe and wonder as he gives to Mary Magdalene, the first witness to the Resurrection, the indescribable honor and privilege of announcing to the apostles that he is risen from the grave.

You turn to Mary, whose dark eyes burn brightly, as though she has been illumined from within. You have never felt as alive as you do at this moment, and you want to rush off with her to find your friends and tell them the amazing news. She does not immediately leave, though. What does she do? What do you do?

Accompany Mary now as she undertakes her sacred mission. Does she realize that she has been singled out to be "the apostle to the apostles"? Does she grasp the magnitude of her powerful leadership role? Or has she so completely let go of her own ego's agenda that she is only thinking of doing what God wants of her? Ask her. How does she respond?

Walking rapidly, you quickly find Peter. Look at Mary and watch how her eyes shine as she tells Peter of the miracle she has just experienced: "I have seen the Lord." As you, too, have seen the Lord, what would you like to add to what Mary Magdalene just said?

Practice 4

———◆———

MEDITATION:
MARY MAGDALENE'S CALLING
IS OUR CALLING

In the Garden of Eden story, God was always close, and men and women could talk with God face-to-face. Beautiful things grew everywhere in perfect ecological harmony; nothing was toxic and nothing died. Here in another garden, beside an empty tomb, some 15 billion years after God created the world that was pure and clean and beautiful, Jesus the Son of God has risen from the dead to start the clock of the universe all over again. The year of his birth is named "1," and the year of his death is named "about 33."

In this new garden of rekindled hope, Jesus has chosen a woman over all of his other disciples and friends to be the one who proclaims the heart-stopping news that death has been overcome and that humankind, too, will rise again. The very sacred task is assigned to Mary Magdalene, who came to Jesus seriously wounded and unhappy years earlier, stayed close, and listened and learned. Long since healed of her woundedness, she is recognized, respected, honored, and lifted up as who she truly is, a revered and cherished lover of God; a sister of wisdom who is sacred to God's son. This modest woman is to announce to the eleven men remaining as apostles—and to us—and to all people for all time—the greatest Christian mystery. And from this time on, all Christians will remember her as "the apostle to the apostles."

The human soul is like this garden where the Fourth Station of Light is set. A place of mystery and wonderful life energies where miracles of growth and blossoming and great surprises occur. A place with a glorious interplay of moistness and dryness; darkness and light; naked earth and greenness; warmth and cold. Our sacred Scriptures have planted in our souls the very same fertile ancient seeds that Jesus planted and tilled in Mary's soul and in those of everyone he touched. As his sayings, parables, and stories taught, some seeds wither and die, some blossom and become beautiful, some open and flower and give fruit.

Waiting for seeds to burst open and vibrant greenness to appear is like Advent, a season of faith and excited anticipation. We nurture and tend the garden to the best of our ability through spiritual practice, and we trust the workings of invisible forces beyond our control, knowing that the God of nurturing love who exercised providential care over the first disciples lives with us today, providing enough moisture, warmth, and light to sustain a lifetime of spiritual growth. We are blessed recipients of divine providential care, but we are responsible for the outcome of the garden, for tending, weeding, pruning, and appropriating grace.

Let us imitate Mary Magdalene by being centered in the garden-space of our souls and proclaiming resurrection faith.

- *What characteristics of a gardener do you see in God?*
- *In what sense do you think of your soul as a garden?*
- *Which of the "fruits of the Spirit" are growing in your soul-garden? The fruits of the Spirit include wisdom, understanding, counsel, strength, knowledge, and awe before God (Isaiah 11:2b), to which the New Testament adds devotion.*
- *Which of these "fruits" (spiritual gifts) need a little more nurturing in your soul?*

Practice 5

———◆———

JOURNAL REFLECTION: SEVEN BLESSINGS

Before Mary Magdalene could grow toward her full potential, she was healed of seven "demons" (Mark 16:9b), meaning wounds, problems, or emotional difficulties of some kind. List in your journal seven occasions in your life when a wound was healed, a problem was solved, or other difficulties were resolved. Conclude with a brief prayer of gratitude for these seven blessings.

Practice 6
———◆———
INSIGHTS AND ILLUMINATIONS

*People from a planet without flowers would think we must be mad
with joy the whole time to have such things about us.*

IRIS MURDOCH

Grow in the garden where you are planted.

SOURCE UNKNOWN

With a garden there is hope.

GRACE FIRTH

God gives the growth.

I CORINTHIANS 3:7B

*The first flower that
blossomed on this earth was
an invitation to the unborn song.*

RABINDRANATH TAGORE

*Oh Adam was a gardener, and God who made him sees
That half a proper gardener's work is done upon his knees.*

RUDYARD KIPLING

*My chief joy is to escape to the attic of the garden house and the little broken
window that looks out over the valley. There in the silence I love the green grass.
The tortured gestures of the apple trees have become part of my prayer. . . . So
much do I love the solitude that when I walk out along the road to the old
barns that stand alone, far from the new buildings, delight begins to overpower
me from head to foot and peace smiles even in the marrow of my bones.*

THOMAS MERTON

What more was there for me to do for my vineyard,
*   That I have not done in it?*
When I looked for it to yield grapes,
*   why did it yield wild grapes?*

ISAIAH 5:4

Be a gardener.
Dig and ditch,
toil and sweat,
and turn the earth upside down
and seek the deepness
and water the plants in time.
Continue this labor
and make sweet floods to run
and noble and abundant fruits
to spring.
Take this food and drink
and carry it to God
as your true worship.

JULIAN OF NORWICH

Practice 7

◆

RELEASING YOUR CREATIVITY: SOUL-GARDENING

1. Take a plain sheet of paper about eight and a half by eleven inches (or larger if you wish), and a pencil or colored pens, pencils, crayons, or paints. You do not need drawing skills in this practice. In your own way, using stick figures if you like, draw a luscious garden that represents your soul. Fill the paper with beautiful things such as flowers and nourishing things such as vegetables and fruits as well as weeds that need to be

removed and places that need pruning. You may wish to include running water, paths, animals, or many other items. *Please complete the drawing before reading paragraph 2 below. The practice will contribute far more to your spiritual growth if you wait than if you read the paragraph now.*

♦   ♦   ♦

2. Now that you have finished drawing your garden, take stock of your garden. Remember that it represents your soul. Notice first what is beautiful (or intended to be beautiful if your drawing skills are limited). What do you love most about your garden? What is growing really well there? What needs some work? How moist is the soil in your garden? Ready to grow and create or dry? Is there enough light and shade? Are there rocky obstacles like anger, meanness, vanity, or self-preoccupation that get in your way? Are there rabbit holes that you or someone else might trip in? What might you donate to a homeless shelter? What else do you see? Be sure to keep your drawing for comparison with future drawings each time you repeat this practice.

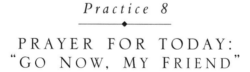

Practice 8

PRAYER FOR TODAY: "GO NOW, MY FRIEND"

My friend,
You are sent to be

>   *Light-bearer*
>   *Bread-giver*

To bear in your eyes the light that has broken
Through the darkness and pain of your journey
So that others may find their way to their destiny:

To carry in your hands the warm bread
You have kneaded in love

So that others may be fed to satiety.
Go now, my friend,

  Give away the candle
  Give away the bread
And be

Candle
Bread.

BROTHER THOMAS MORE PAGE

Practice 9
———◆———
ASKING FOR A SPIRITUAL GIFT

What spiritual gift or blessing would you like to receive today?

Ask, and it will be given to you;
search, and you will find;
knock, and the door will be opened to you.
For the one who asks always receives;
the one who searches always finds;
the one who knocks will always have the door opened to him.

MATTHEW 7:7–8

Practice 10
———◆———
GIVING BACK TO THE COMMUNITY

Think of a simple way to "give back" to life today as an expression of grat-itude for all the blessings you receive.

THE
FIFTH
STATION
OF THE
LIGHT

JESUS APPEARS ON THE ROAD TO EMMAUS

While they were talking and discussing together,
Jesus himself drew near and went with them.

LUKE 24:15

Practice 1

RELAXATION AND CENTERING: MOVING TOWARD STILLNESS

If you know yoga, tai chi, or any other form of body-prayer that helps you to "move toward stillness," spend a few minutes doing this practice now. If you prefer, you may practice the following exercise, "moving toward stillness" in an impromptu way that requires no training or skill at all. You will need music, however, such as chanting or another form of sacred music.

Remain standing and allow yourself to begin performing simple hand and arm movements such as you have seen in modern dance, ballet, tai chi, yoga, or stretching exercises. Then slowly add gentle leg movements and begin moving around in any direction. When you are ready, add head and torso movements until you have given free rein to your whole body.

Continue moving as though you were responding to an invisible invitation. Do not force yourself in any way. Do not think about the next movement or try to plan it. *Follow the inner lead of your soul.* Savor the joy of this freedom for a few minutes, then gradually slow the movements until you become completely still. When you are ready, go on to Practice 2.

Practice 2

READING THE FIFTH STORY

That very day two of them were going to a village named Emmaus, about seven miles from Jerusalem, and talking with each other about all these things that had happened. While they were talking and discussing together, Jesus himself drew near and walked with them. . . . And he said to them, "O how foolish you are! How slow of heart to believe all that the prophets spoke! Was it not necessary that the Christ should suffer these things and enter into his glory?" Then beginning with Moses and all the prophets, he interpreted to them what referred to him in all the scriptures.

LUKE 24:13–15, 25–27

Practice 3

IMAGINING YOURSELF IN THE STORY

Imagine that it is still the first Easter Sunday morning, few people know yet that Jesus is alive, and you are walking along the road from Jerusalem to the village of Emmaus with two devoted disciples, Cleopas and his wife

Mary, the parents of James and Joses.* They are deep in conversation and appear grave. Like most people of their time who are used to life on the road, they wear dusty leather sandals and homespun cloaks over long tunics tied at the waist with a piece of wool. Does Mary wear the typical Middle Eastern veil? How are you dressed?

This roadway will become famous for all time. What is it like today? A hot dusty desert road? Bustling? Broad? Narrow? Rocky? Crowded? How is the weather? Do you see any men? Women? Children? If so, what are they doing? Are there carts? Donkeys? Other animals? What is the landscape like? Do you see any buildings? If so, are they made of wood or stone, or both?

Now a "stranger" comes along and walks with you. You do not realize that it is Jesus, and Mary and Cleopas pour out their hearts to him, telling him how their hopes and dreams were shattered at the death of Jesus. What do you think and feel listening to their outpouring of grief?

The compelling "stranger" responds with wisdom beyond anything you have ever heard, making your heart and mind take flame. He walks with you for several hours, explaining everything, until the whole meaning of Jesus' life and death is crystal clear. What is this like for you? How do you feel? What would you most like to say to this "stranger" who has journeyed with you and given you so much clarity? What does he say in return?

Practice 4

◆

MEDITATION: STRENGTHENING THE SOUL FOR THE JOURNEY

A wonderful transformation takes place in the Fifth Station of Light. When it opens, Cleopas and Mary are walking away from Jerusalem, away

---

The Emmaus disciples were traditionally seen as two men, but recent scholarship suggests that the man here, Cleopas (Luke 24:18), is Clopas (John 19:25), the husband of Mary the mother of James and Joses (Mark 15:40).

from the spiritual community that was forming around Jesus, away from the love, wisdom, and sense of direction that he gave to everyone he met. A week earlier they believed that a whole new future was in their grasp, and now the leader they counted on to take them there is gone. Like ourselves when we are depressed or feel despair, or when we are moving in the wrong direction, they do not realize that God is with them, that he has come to them in the guise of a stranger and is walking at their side on the dusty road to Emmaus and everywhere else the journey leads.

Cleopas and Mary need strength greater than their own to recover from the trauma of Jesus' death and find meaning in their journey, past and future. And that is precisely what transpires through the surprising encounter with the mysterious stranger. He helps them understand that an apparently random and absurd event was a part of a plan with a larger pattern of meaning than the human ego can envision. The event was foreseeable, prophets predicted it, and with the help of God the reasons behind the unfolding of the story are discernible, which makes it possible for the Emmaus couple to lift their heads and walk side by side looking ahead in the same direction, strengthened in wisdom and in faith that the future will be gracious and good.

The road to Emmaus is the story of human existence. God goes before us on the open road with all the answers we need, all the grace and power that is needed to rekindle fire in our hearts and light in our eyes. Sometimes God comes to us disguised as a stranger, and at other times God goes to others disguised as ourselves. Think of the unemployed neighbor who is losing his home. The immigrant working three jobs who looks twice his age from exhaustion and misery. The refugee working in a store who fled a war zone where her parents, husband, and children were killed. Who brings God to whom in such situations?

"We are inclined toward God," as Saint Thomas Aquinas wrote. Our stories begin where all creation begins and lean in the direction that all creation takes. The journey abounds in happiness, delights, rewards, and blessings, yet difficulties and ordeals repeatedly test our strength. We need strength of character to be true to ourselves, moral strength to do what is right, bodily strength to be as healthy as possible, spiritual strength to choose between struggling or letting go. Everyone carries a bag that is a little too heavy, and everyone needs a little more courage than they have.

This is a primary message of the story set on the Emmaus road: The ultimate strength that we cannot summon on our own comes through the grace of the divine presence that creates order out of chaos, makes the apparently random purposeful, causes promises and prophecies to come true, and reminds us to turn and return continually to what is more important than anything else in our lives.

- *Are you aware that other people are seeing God in you?*
- *How do you know when you are going in the wrong direction? What do you do if you need to change course?*
- *Do you see God on the lined faces of the poor? Do you need to work on this? If so, how might you begin?*

Practice 5

JOURNAL REFLECTION:
KNOWING YOUR INNER STRENGTHS

Make a list of ten of your strengths. There are dozens and dozens of possibilities. For example, friendliness, mothering or fathering, faith, professional skills, listening to others with empathy, volunteer work, creativity in a specific area, reliability at work or home, simplicity, fighting for what you believe in, confidence, a pleasant disposition, mindfulness, thoughtful communication, positive thinking, physical or mental or spiritual health, courage, effort to heal the environment, justice work, awareness of the sacred, growing inner life, and so on. Include a new strength that you would like to be open to.

Practice 6

———◆———

INSIGHTS AND ILLUMINATIONS

The secret of strength lies in the quiet mind.

WHITE EAGLE

Events make known the will of God.

CHRISTIAN WISDOM

Send out your light and your truth;
*   let them lead me,*
let them bring me to your holy hill
*   and to your dwelling!*

PSALM 43:3

You are to wander,
entering and departing from
strange villages.
Perhaps you will achieve nothing anywhere.
It may be that the things you carry with you
and your items of trade
find no favor in any place.
But do not turn back. Keep a firm step.
Something you are achieving.
Something the Lord of the Universe
is assigning to you.

ADAPTED FROM "THE COUNSEL OF
A MAYA SAGE," BY CHILAM BALAM,
MAYA PRIEST

Practice 7

RELEASING YOUR CREATIVITY: MAPPING YOUR JOURNEY

Take a large piece of paper, pencils, pens, markers, or crayons and draw a map of your spiritual journey from birth to the present. Use lines to record roads taken and not taken. Use an image or a few words to mark the most important events along the way, as though they were cities on the map.

You may wish to include sacraments that you have received, nourishing relationships, spiritual experiences—such as a beautiful view that gave you a sense of transcendence; losses and dark nights; births and deaths; pilgrimages or other spiritually enriching travels; a few of your spiritual teachers—even a beloved pet who taught you something about unconditional love. If you run out of room, use additional sheets of paper and attach them in book form.

Keep the map (or book of maps or a binder) and continue recording highlights of your journey. You may be surprised at the amount of insight you will gain and be able to use for planning and goal-setting, mindful living, spiritual deepening, service, and so on.

Practice 8

PRAYER FOR TODAY

I have always known
that at last I would
take this road,
but yesterday,

*I did not know
it would be today.*
ANONYMOUS, JAPAN

Practice 9

◆

ASKING FOR A SPIRITUAL GIFT

What spiritual gift or blessing would you like to receive today?

*Ask, and it will be given to you;
search, and you will find;
knock, and the door will be opened to you.
For the one who asks always receives;
the one who searches always finds;
the one who knocks will always have the door opened to him.*
MATTHEW 7:7–8

Practice 10

◆

GIVING BACK
TO THE COMMUNITY

Think of a simple way to "give back" to life today as an expression of gratitude for all the blessings you receive.

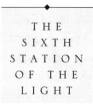

THE RISEN LORD IS RECOGNIZED IN THE BREAKING OF THE BREAD

And their eyes were opened and they recognized him.

LUKE 24:31

Practice 1

RELAXATION AND CENTERING: PICTURING A BELOVED

Begin Practice 1 by sitting in a comfortable, upright position, hands resting in your lap, eyes closed, feet flat on the floor. Allow your spine to be as straight as possible without tightening any muscles.

Picture someone you love. Continue focusing on this person for a moment, allowing the love you feel to flow up freely and fully into your heart. Notice how you feel. Notice the warmth and soft texture that gradually comes over your body. Become aware of the tenderness in your heart, the gentleness in your mental attitude. Continue focusing on this loved person, becoming more and more aware of the fullness and simple happiness and gentleness in your body, soul, and mind. Stay with the image of the beloved until you have fully opened your heart. Then slowly let go of the picture, allowing the love to continue in the absence of an image.

Now your love is not directed at any object. It is pure love—not love "for" anyone. The love that you are feeling now is divine. Rest for a while in the beauty and peace of this awareness. This is the energy to bring to your life today.

Practice 2

READING THE SIXTH STORY

They drew near to the village to which they were going. Jesus appeared to be going further, but they urged him, "Stay with us, for it is nearly evening, and the day is almost over." So he went in to stay with them.

And it happened that while he was at table with them, he took the bread, said the blessing, broke it, and gave it to them. With that, their eyes were opened and they recognized him, but he vanished from their sight. They said to each other, "Were not our hearts burning within us while he talked to us on the way and opened the scriptures to us?"

—LUKE 24:28–32

Practice 3

IMAGINING YOURSELF IN THE STORY

In your imagination, place yourself with Mary and Cleopas and their mysterious companion at dusk as they arrive at a wayside inn on the outskirts of town. Fascinated and inspired by the wisdom of this man who has come so much of the way with them, they cannot bear to part from him and ask him to have dinner with them and stay the night. He nods agreement, and they enter and sit down at a table.

Take a moment to notice what the inn is like, so you will never forget this moment. Is it a simple wooden building with a few rooms or a more lavish establishment made of stone? What is the dining room like? How large is it? Do you sit on chairs or benches? Is there a fireplace? How many people are there? Are there any women and children? What is being served for dinner?

Now watch carefully when bread is brought to the table: The stranger takes it in his hands, blesses it, breaks it, and offers it to you. In a flash of insight, all three of you suddenly realize that this is the Lord. What do you do? What do you say?

Practice 4

MEDITATION:
BREAKING BREAD TOGETHER

The divine spark in the soul can never be extinguished. It may burn brighter on some days and barely glow on others, but the ember is always there, ready to be kindled and burst into flames. In the Fifth Station of Light, we journeyed on the road to Emmaus with Mary and Cleopas, whose discouragement was short-lived because of a powerful encounter with the living God. The remedy came when they grasped the meaning of the Scriptures, when they listened to the words of Scripture as they never had before, and heard a message they had never heard before. A new depth of wisdom was being revealed to them, and as they listened, the words sank in deeply and their hearts began to "burn within them."

A spirit of passionate caring, desire, bliss, and certainty made them feel alive again, as they had before betrayal and ruin took away the person in whom they had placed all their hope. A mysterious traveler explains to them the meaning of the events they have gone through, and the very fire they feel as he speaks is a hint that this glorious stranger is the friend they have lost. What is certain, his words set fire to their whole being—body, mind, and soul—as only Jesus could.

Only when the stranger performs the same sacred ritual as before the Last Supper—picking up the large loaf of bread, saying the blessing, breaking it into pieces, and passing a piece to each of them—do they finally awaken and realize who is with them. We imagine Mary and Cleopas jumping up to hug Jesus just as he disappears, as in the Third Station when he refused to let Mary Magdalene cling to him in the garden by the empty tomb. But they have recognized him in the breaking of the bread—as we ourselves do by participating in the Eucharistic meal.

Bread is a universal source of nourishment—sometimes the only source of nourishment on the tables of the poor. Freshly baked bread is a delight to make, to look at, to smell, touch, and taste; good for health; good for sharing and giving away. And for the People of God, bread is even more than something wonderful to ingest and assimilate, although it is all that. Bread is also a symbol, an ultimately significant, rich, evocative symbol of the presence of the Christ, the soul's sustenance. "Christ is the bread of life" (John 6:35). Christ dies and rises to assuage the ravenous spiritual hunger of humankind through the mystery of consecrated bread.

• *How is the transformation of bread dough through the addition of yeast like the Christian life?*
• *If the seed does not die, wheat cannot be grown for the making of bread. Is that a good metaphor for the Christian life? How?*

Practice 5

———◆———

JOURNAL REFLECTION: FEASTING

You may wish to do this exercise in your journal without any intention of carrying it out in daily life.

The classic film *Babette's Feast* showed how gathering around a table to eat a meal together can overcome alienation with healing and redemption. In *Tortilla Soup,* sharing meals at the family table nurtured many dimensions of human connectedness, among them love, laughter, conflicts, and conversations. Make an imaginative plan in your journal today for a feast that could be shared with family members or friends in a spirit of celebration. Write out a delicious menu to delight all the senses and a plan to bring out the sacredness of the occasion with a simple ritual.

The ritual should nurture the guests' connectedness to one another. You may wish to invite guests to bring sacred poems and prayers to read between courses; play appropriate music; incorporate candles, flowers, or incense; if a dancer is among the guests, you may wish to open or close with a sacred dance.

Practice 6

———◆———

INSIGHTS AND ILLUMINATIONS

Bless our hearts
to hear in the
breaking of bread
the song of the universe.
REV. JOHN B. GIULIANI

Why did I not recognize You when I first opened my eyes on the earth?

SUFI WISDOM

When you pray, shut your eyes for a moment and try to concentrate your spiritual powers. If your mind wanders, open your eyes and focus briefly on an icon or candle flame. Concentrating on prayer this way, you will experience within yourself that spiritual warmth that comes from Christ and fills one's whole being with peace and joy.

SAINT SERAPHIM OF SERAVOV

Don't you sense me, ready to break into being at your touch?

RAINER MARIA RILKE

You have come my beloved,
The clouds are gone,
The wind is silent,
The sun appears,
And the trees are green.

TINH THUY

I thank my God every time I remember you. In all my prayers for all of you, I always pray with joy because of your partnership in the good news from the first until now, being confident of this, that he who began a good work in you will carry it on to completion until the day of Christ Jesus.

PHILIPPIANS 1:8–10

Practice 7

RELEASING YOUR CREATIVITY: SEEING GOD IN THE BREAKING OF BREAD

Think of ways to deepen your spiritual journey today by celebrating the sacredness of mealtimes. For instance, you could begin with a prayer that recognizes God's presence in the food and honors the long chain of people who worked to bring it to your table: farmers, truckers, factory workers, stock people, salesclerks, and many others.

Make an effort to eat only healthy foods that are as free as possible of toxicities. Eat very slowly, savoring every bite, chewing for a long time, enjoying the different tastes, smells, colors, temperatures, and textures. You will enhance the spirituality of the meal by eating no more than you need to supply the right amount of nutrients that will adequately energize your body. It is best not to read or write or do anything else while you are striving to make mealtime part of your spiritual practice. Pay attention to the way your awareness changes when you eat this way.

Practice 8

PRAYER FOR TODAY: "OUR FATHER"

Our Father,
who art in heaven
hallowed be thy name
thy kingdom come
thy will be done
on earth as it is in heaven.

Give us this day
our daily bread
and forgive us our trespasses
as we forgive those who trespass against us
and deliver us from evil.
    Amen.

Practice 9

◆

ASKING FOR A SPIRITUAL GIFT

What spiritual gift or blessing would you like to receive today?

Ask, and it will be given to you;
search, and you will find;
knock, and the door will be opened to you.
For the one who asks always receives;
the one who searches always finds;
the one who knocks will always have the door opened to him.
                    —MATTHEW 7:7–8

Practice 10

◆

GIVING BACK
TO THE COMMUNITY

Think of a simple way to "give back" to life today as an expression of gratitude for all the blessings you receive.

THE RISEN LORD APPEARS TO THE COMMUNITY OF DISCIPLES

And Jesus said to them, "Why are you so agitated?"
LUKE 24:38A

Practice 1

RELAXATION AND CENTERING: BREATHING IN PEACE, BREATHING OUT STRESS

Begin your practice today by sitting in a comfortable, upright position, hands resting in your lap, eyes closed, feet flat on the floor. Allow your spine to be as straight as possible without tightening any muscles.

Place your attention on your breathing. Simply watch the inhalations and exhalations come and go gently like the waves on a beach, until you have begun centering. Now imagine yourself breathing in "peace" with every inhalation and breathing out "fear" with every exhalation. Say silently and very slowly to yourself as you inhale, "I breathe in peace," and as you exhale, say equally slowly, "I breathe out stress."

With each inhalation, picture the breath filling your entire body with peace. Feel it flow up to the top of your head, down to the tips of your fingers, all the way down to the toes. Notice how full and whole you feel as every cell in your body fills with peacefulness.

As you exhale, imagine yourself breathing out stress. Allow tension to wash out of your body, a little more with each out-breath. Each time you exhale, picture the tightness in your muscles being released. Feel stress stream down from the top of the head, up from the fingertips and toe-tips, and out of your body with the out-breath.

Continue for a few minutes. The breaths will become longer and more tranquil, the intervals between them will lengthen, and your entire body and soul will sink further and further into your natural state of blissful peace.

Practice 2

♦

READING THE SEVENTH STORY

They were still talking about all this when Jesus himself stood among them and said to them: "Peace be with you!" In a state of alarm and fright, they thought they were seeing a ghost. But he said to them, "Why are you so agitated, and why are these doubts rising in your hearts? Look at my hands and my feet; yes, it is I indeed. Touch me and see for yourselves; a ghost has no flesh and bones as you can see I have."

LUKE 24:36–39

Practice 3

---◆---

IMAGINING YOURSELF
IN THE STORY

In your imagination, find yourself sitting with the disciples in the Upper Room. What is it like for you to be back here in the very room where the Last Supper was held? Look around and feel the sacredness and significance of this room. You will be here again on the day when "Doubting Thomas" embraces faith, and again on Pentecost. Notice all the details you can: the size, colors, materials that the floor, walls, and ceiling are made of; what the windows are like; if they are opened, curtained, offer a view. What are the furnishings like? What sounds do you hear? Do you detect any aromas, like the smell of food cooking? What else? Whom do you recognize in the community?

Your musings are interrupted by Mary and Cleopas, who have rushed back from Emmaus and burst into the room with the amazing news that Jesus has appeared to them. Listen to the wonder and elation in their voices as they share how Jesus spent hours with them on the road to Emmaus, telling them marvelous things. Someone else says, "The Lord has risen indeed, and has appeared to Simon" (Luke 24:34). You share their joy, but many of the other disciples do not. To the contrary, many look unconvinced. Are you surprised? What emotions do you think they are feeling?

Just then, Jesus appears in your midst. What is it like for you when someone shouts out, "It's a ghost!"? Now watch how Jesus soothes and calms everyone. Notice the infinite tenderness as he asks, "Why are you so agitated?" A hush comes over the room, and he adds: "I am here with you, I myself. There is no reason to be so distressed."

Can you feel tension and negative emotions dissipating in the room? Turn to the person nearest you to express what is in your heart. What do you say? What does this person say back to you?

Practice 4

◆

MEDITATION: "DIVINE PSYCHOTHERAPY"

In the Seventh Station of Light, we meet anxious men and women who have heard about the empty tomb but have not yet themselves encountered the living God and remain unconvinced about the Resurrection. Without God in their hearts, they are afraid, sad, doubtful, discouraged, like ourselves when we lose sight of what we care about most. But Jesus, like a loving mother protecting her small children, invites them to come close to him for comfort and reassurance. His disturbed disciples need to know that he is there for them and is the same as always, not merely a projection of their own minds, but a presence of love that melts away painful fears.

What transpires between the agitated disciples and the risen Lord is like deep prayer. Only a few words are spoken, but they are enough to restore the broken connection with the Divine while stilling and freeing the mind of anxiety. In loving communion with God, the heart reopens, awareness of the mind's spaciousness returns, and the body relaxes, as when we contemplate the beauty of nature and feel one with the ocean, a tree, or a smooth white stone.

Often when we go to God in the silence of contemplation, "divine psychotherapy" occurs.* We are taken beyond the false self to the person we really want to be and already are. At such times we are one with ourselves, unconflicted and unself-critical. One with humankind, nonjudgmental and unresentful. One with the source of all life, free and strong. Then there is no need to hide what we fear, what we want to forget, or what we dislike about ourselves. It can all come safely, through grace, into the light of God. Dark emotions, painful memories, traumas, and other blocks to freedom can be released and given back to God.

---

* The term "divine psychotherapy" comes from the Trappist monk Thomas Keating, who worked with two other monks at Saint Joseph's Abbey in Spencer, Massachusetts, Fathers Basil Pennington and William Meninger, to revive the ancient tradition of Centering Prayer in our time.

• *What fear (or other strong emotion) do you most need to release and give to God?*
• *What is the opportunity hidden in this fear/emotion?*
• *If a problem is creating the fear/emotion, would contemplative prayer help you to let go of the emotion even though the problem isn't yet solved?*

Practice 5
<hr>

JOURNAL REFLECTION: RELEASING FEAR

List in your journal five occasions in your life when you overcame fear. What methods did you use to release those fears? How do you think it would help to use contemplative prayer the next time you need to let go of fear?

Practice 6
<hr>

INSIGHTS AND ILLUMINATIONS

The boat people said that every time their small boats were caught in storms, they knew their lives were in danger. But if one person on the boat could keep calm and not panic, that was a great help for everyone. People would listen to him or her and keep serene, and there was a chance for the boat to survive the danger. Our Earth is like a small boat. Compared with the rest of the cosmos, it is a small boat indeed, and it is in danger of sinking. We need such a person to inspire us with calm confidence, to tell us what to do. Who is that person?

The Mahayana Buddhist [scriptures] tell us that you are that person. If you are yourself, if you are your best, then you are that person. Only with such a person—calm, lucid, aware—will our situation improve.

I wish you good luck. Please be yourself. Please be that person.

THICH NHAT HANH

Come to me all you who labor
and are overburdened,
and I will give you rest.
Shoulder my yoke and learn from me,
for I am gentle and humble in heart,
and you will find rest in your souls.
Yes, my yoke is easy and my burden is light.

MATTHEW 11:28–30

May I be the doctor and the medicine
And may I be the nurse
For all sick beings in the world
Until everyone is healed.

FROM A PRAYER OF SHANTIDEVA

Peace I leave with you.
My own peace I give to you.
A peace the world cannot give; this is my gift to you.
Do not let your hearts be troubled or afraid.

JOHN 14:27

May I be happy.
May I be peaceful.
May I be loving.
May I be safe.
May you be happy.
May you be peaceful.
May you be loving.
May you be safe.
May all beings be happy.

May all beings be peaceful.
May all beings be loving.
May all beings be safe.
TRADITIONAL BUDDHIST PRAYER

Practice 7

─────◆─────

RELEASING YOUR CREATIVITY: BRINGING BEAUTY INTO THE DAY

Look for a way to add beauty to the day. Watch to see how enriching your own soul-life with beauty affects people you are connected to.

Practice 8

─────◆─────

PRAYER FOR TODAY

Let nothing upset you,
Let nothing frighten you.
Everything is changing;
God alone is changeless.
Patience attains the goal.
Who has God lacks nothing;
God alone fills all their needs.

TERESA OF ÁVILA

Practice 9

————◆————

ASKING FOR A SPIRITUAL GIFT

What spiritual gift or blessing would you like to receive today?

Ask, and it will be given to you;
search, and you will find;
knock, and the door will be opened to you.
For the one who asks always receives;
the one who searches always finds;
the one who knocks will always have the door opened to him.

MATTHEW 7:7–8

Practice 10

————◆————

GIVING BACK
TO THE COMMUNITY

Think of a simple way to "give back" to life today as an expression of gratitude for all the blessings you receive.

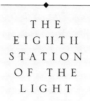

THE RISEN LORD GIVES THE POWER TO FORGIVE

He breathed on them and said, "Receive the Holy Spirit."
JOHN 20:22

Practice 1

RELAXATION AND CENTERING: EMPTYING THE MIND

Begin your practice today by sitting in a comfortable, upright position, hands resting in your lap, eyes closed, feet flat on the floor. Allow your spine to be as straight as possible without tightening any muscles.

If you have a home altar, sit (or kneel) close to it, facing it. Focus your eyes on an item that is sacred to you. A candle flame, flower, picture, a symbol of something precious to you or something you value, say a stone to symbolize strength. Continue focusing your attention on the object. When a thought interrupts your concentration, imagine it rising upward into the sky like a bubble, and gently bring your attention back to the object. Allow any distractions that arise to float upward like bubbles. Become aware—as one thought after another appears, floats away, and disappears—that your mind is emptying and you are entering into the sacred spaciousness of the soul, free and close to God. Rest for a moment in the joyful experience.

Practice 2

———◆———

READING THE EIGHTH STORY

> *Jesus said to the disciples, "Peace be with you. As the Father has sent me, so am I sending you." After saying this, he breathed on them, and said: "Receive the Holy Spirit. For those whose sins you forgive, they are forgiven."*
>
> JOHN 20:21–23

Practice 3

———◆———

IMAGINING YOURSELF IN THE STORY

To pray with your whole self—body, soul, and mind—allow your senses to come to life through the following practice, entering personally into the sacred event as though it were taking place right now and you were there.

Locate yourself again with the apostles in the Upper Room, where a well-to-do follower of Jesus hosted a Seder supper for him last Thursday. Jesus has been in the room for a while conversing and interacting with everyone. You notice how strongly his presence has changed the energy in the room. What is the difference? Is it more intense and expectant? More sacred and loving? What is it like to be in that charged environment with him? How are you feeling? Excited? Awed? Allow your physical senses free rein to see, hear, smell, touch details of everything there in order to fix in your mind permanently the scene that is about to unfold. It is like a mini liturgical drama or a sacred ritual in three parts:

- *First, your beloved Teacher breathes on you.*
- *Second, in a strong and authoritative tone of voice, he says: "Receive the Holy Spirit."*
- *Third, he concludes the sacred ritual by making a puzzling connection between breathing his Spirit into you and forgiveness. If you forgive the sins of any, he proclaims, they are forgiven.*

This is not the first time that you have seen Jesus perform a symbolic action like an Old Testament prophet, as when he wrote cryptically on the ground to make a point. But this time it is different, more mystical, harder to interpret, like a mystery rite. Do you understand what he has done? Can you grasp the importance? Look around at the apostles. Do they seem bewildered? Are you going to ask Jesus for an explanation? Do you prefer to wait for him to make his meaning clear? Select someone in the room with whom you would like to ponder what just took place and open a conversation. What do you say? How does that person respond?

Practice 4

MEDITATION: THE POWER OF FORGIVENESS

Read the following words very slowly, pausing as often as you wish to reflect.

In the Eighth Station of Light, Jesus offers a teaching so important, so life-giving and nourishing, that he not only speaks about it, he enacts it. Through the symbolic action of breathing, the most ordinary and natural act of our everyday reality, he gives the disciples a teaching in what the

Spirit is like. Through this simple gesture that the world has never forgotten and will never forget, the risen Lord gives his followers an experiential awareness that the Holy Spirit exists within us and among us like the air we breathe. Just as the process of inhaling and exhaling sustains the life of the body, so the flow of the Spirit gives life to the soul. Life without breath is impossible, and life without Spirit dries up and dies.

The scriptural passage you read today concerns one of the Spirit's most precious gifts, the power of forgiveness, the ability to forgive and be forgiven. We are empowered just because we breathe to receive the forgiveness of God, to forgive the people who hurt us, and to ask for and accept forgiveness from the people we hurt, no matter how unintentional the injury. Because the risen Lord gave his life for us, we are forgiven always and unconditionally by God, even before we do something wrong. We are accepted, we are loved through all eternity, we are blessed and graced by a sacramental life that bestows the joy and peace of forgiveness.

It is wrong to harm the soul of another person. That is a sacred truth, the first moral lesson that elders teach to the young, a message continually on Jesus' lips. Yet many relationships fail in our homes, schools, offices, and countries because we hurt one another's souls. Wounds occur every day to trust, hope, security, self-esteem, the invaluable virtue of pride in who and what one is, in self-love, and countless other good soul-qualities. But in the life of faith and love, through the power of the Spirit that has been given to us permanently, we are able to forgive one another "seventy times seven," as Jesus taught (Matthew 18:22). For reconciliation is part of our sacramental life.

Jesus forgave his executioners on the grounds that "They know not what they do." In the midst of the ultimate injustice and physical pain of his Passion, he prayed for his enemies because they had no idea who he was or who they were themselves, nor did they have the remotest insight into the magnitude of what Jesus was accomplishing for humankind. It was their ignorance that he forgave. They ought to have known better, but they did not. And from his divine point of view, that was reason enough to forgive.

The mystical author Andrew Harvey tells a beautiful story about the Dalai Lama, the titular head of the Tibetan Buddhists. Andrew was meeting with him when a monk came in and handed the Dalai Lama a message that caused him to weep for several minutes. After regaining his composure, the Dalai Lama whispered to the people present: "Last night, the Chinese tortured and murdered over a hundred of our monks and nuns. Now let us pray for the Chinese."

- *There is great joy and health and dignity to be found in restoring a broken connection through forgiveness. Is there someone whom you would like to forgive or from whom you would like to ask forgiveness?*
- *Do you aspire to the extraordinary degree of forgiveness that the Dalai Lama exemplifies? Would you like to? What would you need to let go of in yourself to be more forgiving?*

Practice 5

JOURNAL REFLECTION: LEARNING TO CHERISH

Write in your journal the names of three people whom you cherish and three people whom you do not at all cherish. Remind yourself that we are all connected: We are all members of the human family. Resolve that you will cultivate an attitude of cherishing in your heart and extend that attitude to everyone as well as to animal friends and nature and especially to those three people whom you do not cherish. Write down three occasions during the week when you can practice this attitude toward people you do not know, say clerks, mail deliverers, table servers, attendants, and so on.

Practice 6

———◆———

INSIGHTS AND ILLUMINATIONS

God is delighted to watch your soul enlarge.

MEISTER ECKHART

There is an unseen
presence we honor,
that gives the gifts.

RUMI

When we look into our hearts and begin to discover what is confused and
what is brilliant, what is bitter and what is sweet, it isn't just ourselves that
we're discovering. We're discovering the universe.

PEMA CHODRON

Peter came up and said to him, "Lord, how often will my brother sin against
me, and I forgive him? As many as seven times?" Jesus said to him, "I do
not say to you seven times, but seventy times seven."

MATTHEW 18:21–22

You may call God love,
you may call God goodness,
but the best name for God is
compassion.

MEISTER ECKHART

We all make many mistakes.

JAMES 3:2A

Confess your sins to one another, and pray for one another,
that you may be healed.

JAMES 5:16A

Speak words of faith.
TRADITIONAL

Judge not, and you will not be judged;
condemn not, and you will not be condemned;
forgive, and you will be forgiven.

LUKE 6:37

Practice 7

◆

RELEASING YOUR CREATIVITY: CREATING A FORGIVENESS PROCESS

Think of a personal relationship—or a relationship between nations—that has been wounded and could be healed by forgiveness. Create a forgiveness process for remedying this situation, listing the specific steps that need to be taken. Here are a few sample steps that you may wish to include:

- *Pray for a greater desire to forgive;*
- *Set guidelines for the process, such as mandatory kindness;*
- *Try to understand others' positions;*
- *Elicit compassion for the wounding person by imagining the hard part of their life;*
- *Determine if a third party like a counselor or consultant should be involved;*
- *Reflect on the likely outcome of e-mails, face-to-face meetings, apologies, humor, and other ways of connecting before using them;*
- *Pray for the person who hurt you;*
- *Consider if the wiser course might be to forgo direct contact with the other person and do the inner forgiveness work of prayer and reflec-*

tion; this requires your letting go of any remaining attachment to this person, leaving him or her in God's hands;
• *Receive the sacrament of reconciliation.*

Practice 8
◆

PRAYER FOR TODAY

*If I have hurt or harmed anyone knowingly or unknowingly,
  I ask their forgiveness.
If I have hurt or harmed you knowingly or unknowingly,
  I ask your forgiveness.*

*If anyone has hurt or harmed me knowingly or unknowingly, I forgive them.
If you have hurt or harmed me knowingly or unknowingly, I forgive you.
For all the ways I have hurt or harmed myself knowingly or unknowingly,
  I offer forgiveness.*

BUDDHIST FORGIVENESS MEDITATION

Practice 9
◆

ASKING FOR A SPIRITUAL GIFT

What spiritual gift or blessing would you like to receive today?

*Ask, and it will be given to you;
search, and you will find;
knock, and the door will be opened to you.
For the one who asks always receives;*

the one who searches always finds;
the one who knocks will always have the door opened to him.

MATTHEW 7:7–8

Practice 10

———◆———

GIVING BACK
TO THE COMMUNITY

Think of a simple way to "give back" to life today as an expression of gratitude for all the blessings you receive.

THE RISEN

LORD STRENGTHENS

THE FAITH OF THOMAS

Jesus said to Thomas: "Do not be unbelieving; but believe."
JOHN 20:27B

Practice 1

RELAXATION AND CENTERING: BREATHING IN TRUST, BREATHING OUT FEAR

Begin your practice today by sitting in a comfortable, upright position, hands resting in your lap, eyes closed, feet flat on the floor. Allow your spine to be as straight as possible without tightening any muscles.

Your relaxation practice for today is a variation of the relaxation practice for the Seventh Way of Light, when you breathed in "peace" and breathed out "stress." Today you will inhale "trust" and exhale "fear." Or if you wish, substitute two other qualities that better fit your needs today, say "forgiveness" during the in-breath and "guilt" during the out-breath. Or inhale "clinging" and exhale "letting go." Pairing "anger" and "serenity" is another possibility, as is "anxiety" and "serenity," and so on.

Take the customary posture for Practice 1, and begin by observing your breath. Allow the inhalations and exhalations to come and go gently, quietly, naturally, like waves on a beach. After half a minute or so, when you are ready, begin breathing in "trust" with every inhalation, and breathing out "fear" with every exhalation. As you inhale, say silently and very slowly, "I breathe in trust," and as you exhale, say just as slowly, "I breathe out fear."

With each inhalation, picture the breath carrying trust throughout your entire body. Feel it flow up to the top of your head, down to the fingertips, all the way down to the toes. Notice how full and whole you feel as the breath brings trust into every cell. As you exhale, allow fear to wash out of your entire body, to flow down from the top of the head, up from the fingertips and toe-tips, and out with the exhalation. Picture fear draining out of every cell in the body and washing entirely out of you.

Continue for a few minutes. The breaths will become longer and more tranquil, the intervals between them will lengthen, and your entire body and soul will sink further and further into your natural state of blissful peace.

Practice 2

———◆———

READING THE NINTH STORY

Now Thomas, one of the twelve, called the Twin, was not with them when Jesus came. So the other disciples told him, "We have seen the Lord." But he said to them, "Unless I see the mark of the nails in his hands and put my finger into the nail marks and put my hand into his side, I will not believe."
Eight days later, his disciples were again in the house, and Thomas was with them. The doors were shut, but Jesus came and stood among them, and said, "Peace be with you." Then he said to Thomas, "Put

*your finger here and see my hands; and bring your hand and put it
into my side, and do not be unbelieving, but believe."
Thomas answered him, "My Lord and my God!" Jesus said to him,
"Do you believe because you see me? Blessed are those who do not see
and yet believe."*

JOHN 20:24–29

Practice 3

———◆———

IMAGINING YOURSELF IN THE STORY

*To pray with your whole self—body, soul, and mind—allow your senses to
come to life through the following practice, entering personally into the sacred
event as though it were taking place right now and you were there.*

It is now eight days since the first Easter, and you are again with the disciples from Jesus' inner circle in your preferred meeting place, the Upper
Room. This spacious room provides a quiet, safe place where your small
community can pray and continue reflecting on the meaning of Jesus'
teachings and post-Resurrection visits while trying to discern what you are
meant to do next. By now, all of you have seen and dialogued with the
risen Lord except for Thomas, who is there with you today.

Look around the room. How does it look today? What time is it? What
do you see from the small windows? What food and beverages are on the
long table? Notice all the aromas, sounds, colors, textures in the room.
How does it feel to be there again with cherished friends?

Become aware of Thomas dominating the scene. He refuses to believe
that Jesus is truly alive. Having witnessed the many signs of Jesus' divine
power during the years of the public ministry, he protests that he would
have to see the scars on Jesus' body before believing that he has survived
death. How would you describe Thomas's attitude? What kind of pain is
he feeling? How does he look? Go over and speak to him; be compassion-

ate. What do you say? What does he reply? What is the tone of his voice? The look on his face? His body language?

Just then, Jesus appears right beside you and speaks gently to Thomas until he is centered in his heart. Then Jesus tells Thomas: Trust! You notice the hush that has come over the room as Jesus shows Thomas the scars where his wounds have been healing this past week. Thomas gasps and prays, "My Lord and my God!" Did he throw himself down on his knees when he said that? How does it feel to see Thomas finally awaken? What would you like to say to Thomas now? How does he respond?

Practice 4

◆

MEDITATION:
SEEING WHAT IS HIDDEN

Read the following words very slowly, pausing as often as you wish to reflect.

In the Ninth Station of Light, Thomas is searching, seeking, struggling to find the Resurrection faith that has given his friends so much joy. He is longing to believe that Jesus is risen from the dead, but nothing his friends have said to him has proved convincing. Like ourselves when we doubt, he is looking for more than reasons, opinions, and arguments to help him make the great leap to faith.

The word "faith" is related to a word that means "giving one's heart to." And the word "belief" is related to the German word *belieben,* which contains the word *liebe,* or love. The faith that Thomas is looking for is a vision of the heart that mingles experiential awareness of infinite love with a loving attitude of trust. This is the faith that Thomas seeks.

It is the same with us. We want beliefs that we can ride to the center of our souls in order to communicate directly with the Divine. We want to know the Holy One in wordless prayer at our own depths, to connect and reconnect with God in an intimate relationship. And that is a gift of Resurrection faith. Our spiritual feelings and religious insights, our learning and prayer, affirm what Jesus taught and what the Scriptures claim: The Spirit of the Christ is with us, the same yesterday, today, and tomorrow, journeying with us through the grand adventure of life with all its delights and huge upheavals.

The ego is content with superficialities, appearances, the exterior of things, as though jewels grew on the outside of the mountain and not deep inside. But the spiritual self sees beyond appearances to what is hidden. There is more going on in every person, every event, and every being in creation than we can ever fully appreciate. There are so many motives behind every decision made that it is almost impossible to know exactly what the "real reason" is, and it is totally impossible to know the motives that underlie another person's behavior. As a fictional character in a short story says of her husband after many years of marriage, she never could "get under the rock of his reasons." So much lies beneath the surface of things that the best eyes and hearts and intellects are not enough. We need also to trust.

"God reveals and God conceals." Some things are made known and some things remain unknown. But the gift of faith is a spiritual gift for seeing more and more, a gift of inner vision that can broaden and brighten almost endlessly. It is as though our faith conferred a new set of eyes with an almost unlimited field of vision, and the more we use them, the farther we see. The more we pray, the more we understand.

> • *There is a nobility and dignity and joy to Christian faith that elicits unconditional, lifelong commitment among millions of people all over the world. Do you have a sense of permanent commitment?*
> • *If not, how could you strengthen your commitment? Would a more conscious experience of God help, say through deep prayer or contemplating beauty in nature? (Many other ways are suggested throughout this book.)*

Practice 5
◆

JOURNAL REFLECTION: WHAT STORIES DO YOU REMEMBER?

Mention five stories, psalms, or prayers from our sacred Scriptures that have nourished your faith (such as the Creation, the Twenty-third Psalm, the Annunciation to Mary, her Magnificat, Jesus' birth, his baptism, the Prodigal Son, Healing of the Paralytic, the Lilies of the Fields, or the Beatitudes). There are hundreds more to choose from. Explore in your journal how one of these stories has supported your faith or how it has helped you in times of doubt. You may wish to respond to the following questions:

- *Which stories or psalms or prayers still your mind when you are agitated?*
- *Which energize you when you are feeling discouraged?*
- *Which increase your awareness of the presence of God?*
- *How else have they helped?*

Practice 6
◆

INSIGHTS AND ILLUMINATIONS

I had heard of you by the hearing of the ear,
but now my eyes see you.

JOB 42:5

Now we see only reflections in a mirror, but then we will see face to face.

I CORINTHIANS 13:12

Let me know you, O you who know me; then shall
I know even as I am known.

SAINT AUGUSTINE

Who believes in me has life everlasting.

JOHN 6:47

Practice 7

◆

RELEASING YOUR CREATIVITY: WHAT IS YOUR IMAGE FOR GOD?

Most people use images for God, often images from nature. God is portrayed as, say, a mountain or an ocean. Does a particular image come to mind when you think about God? Or do you have a number of images? You may wish to skim the stories of the Way of Light for ideas. Select one image for journaling today. Ask yourself: Why does this specific image connote God to you? What characteristics of God does it suggest to you?

Practice 8

◆

PRAYER FOR TODAY

Lord, make me an instrument of your peace.
Where there is hatred, let me sow love;
Where there is injury, pardon;
Where there is doubt, faith;
Where there is despair, hope;
Where there is darkness, light;

Where there is sadness, joy.
O Divine Mater, grant that I may not seek so much
To be consoled as to console,
To be understood as to understand.
To be loved as to love;
For it is in giving that we receive;
It is in pardoning that we are pardoned;
It is in dying that we are born to eternal life.

SAINT FRANCIS OF ASSISI

Practice 9

♦

ASKING FOR A SPIRITUAL GIFT

What spiritual gift or blessing would you like to receive today?

Ask, and it will be given to you;
search, and you will find;
knock, and the door will be opened to you.
For the one who asks always receives;
the one who searches always finds;
the one who knocks will always have the door opened to him.

MATTHEW 7:7–8

Practice 10

♦

GIVING BACK TO THE COMMUNITY

Think of a simple way to "give back" to life today as an expression of gratitude for all the blessings you receive.

JESUS TELLS PETER,
"FEED MY SHEEP"

Jesus said to Simon Peter, "Feed my sheep."
JOHN 21:17

Practice 1

❖

RELAXATION AND CENTERING:
LETTING GO OF THOUGHTS

Begin your practice today by sitting in a comfortable, upright position, hands resting in your lap, eyes closed, feet flat on the floor. Allow your spine to be as straight as possible without tightening any muscles.

Take three long, deep breaths to begin centering. Focus your attention on your mind, seeing it as a vast open sky where thoughts flow gently by like clouds. The mind is spacious, and the thoughts are peaceful. Allow all worries and anxiety to flow away in these clouds. There is nothing to be anxious about, no problem that worry or anxiety will solve. Continue focusing on the spacious mind without resisting the stream of thoughts. Notice how these thoughts come up into your awareness, then float on toward the horizon of the mind. Let them come up, and let them go on.

Rest for a minute or two in the peace of being the observer, not the thinker. Enjoy the freedom of not being in control.

If a thought returns or persists in returning, you may wish to dispel it by briefly jotting it down on a slip of paper, then returning to your meditation.

Practice 2

---◆---

READING THE TENTH STORY

When they had finished breakfast,
Jesus said to Simon Peter,
*   "Simon, son of John, do you love me more than these others do?"*
Peter answered,
*   "Yes, Lord, you know I love you."*
Jesus said to him,
*   "Feed my lambs."*

A second time,
Jesus said to him,
*   "Simon, son of John, do you love me?"*
He replied,
*   "Yes, Lord, you know I love you."*
Jesus said to him,
*   "Look after my sheep."*

Then he said to him a third time,
*   "Simon, son of John, do you love me?"*
Peter was upset that he asked a third time, "Do you love me?"
And said,

"Lord, you know everything; you know I love you."
Jesus said to him,
"Feed my sheep."

JOHN 21:15–17

Practice 3

---◆---

IMAGINING YOURSELF IN THE STORY

To pray with your whole self—body, soul, and mind—allow your senses to come to life through the following practice, entering personally into the sacred event as though it were taking place right now and you were there.

It is early in the morning in ancient Palestine by the Sea of Tiberias, where the risen Christ stands on the shore of the sea cooking breakfast over an open fire. He has just guided the apostles to catch a large school of fish and now invites them to come in to shore and eat with him.

Imagine that you are there enjoying this breakfast with the remaining eleven apostles and Jesus. Allow your eyes to slowly scan the horizon all around you. Notice first the beauty of the Sea of Tiberias. How does it look at this time of day? Is it blue, or green, or black at this time of day? What is the sky like? Are any birds flying overhead? What do you see in other directions, an open space of desert and low mountains with few people in sight, or a busier landscape with roads, houses, people, animals, and plants? What sounds do you hear? Voices? Birds calling? Donkeys braying? Other animals?

The aroma of hot food increases your hunger and your gaze returns to the breakfast scene. What is it like? How is the food being served? Do you sit on the ground? What colors and textures do you see there? What odors intrigue you? What foods and beverage are you eating?

Now look around the circle at each of the apostles and notice the love on their faces. What other expressions do you see? Awe and reverence? Devotion? Simple happiness? Peace? Pay close attention to Peter. How does he stand out in the group? How is he different from the others?

Now your eyes settle on your beloved Teacher. Here are the deepest eyes you have ever seen. What do they convey to you? What do you discern in his facial expression and body language? Are there any signs that he is about to give one of his most beautiful and sacred teachings? How does he get everyone's attention? Listen to the incomparable tone of his voice as he begins to speak: What is it like? Sit quietly now and open your heart as wide as possible to receive all that you can of his great self-giving wisdom and love.

Practice 4

◆

MEDITATION: SACRED LOVE

Read the following words very slowly, pausing as often as you wish to reflect.

You have arrived at one of the most moving and beautiful stories in the Christian Scriptures. It begins with Christ calling to his closest disciples as he calls to us, "Come and eat your meal," a meal that he himself has prepared. The scene reminds us of many other images of food, cooking, and eating in his stories, as when he told his disciples, "You are the salt of the earth" (Matthew 5:13), or when he compared the reign of God to "yeast" (Matthew 13:33). Or the time he fed a crowd of people with five loaves of bread and two fish (Mark 6:30–44). Always both the body and the soul are nourished.

On this day, when breakfast is finished, Jesus turns to Peter and opens a conversation that many people two thousand years later know by heart. Notice that the dialogue takes place at the sea, a striking symbol of deep, vast beauty and mystery, like our own souls, and like the luminous darkness of God's womb, the source of life.

A sea, which teems with colorful fish, bright rock formations, plants, and many unknown life-forms, reminds us of the motherhood of God and the divine love that from all eternity creates, nurtures, and renews.

At the Tenth Station, this world-transforming story teaches humankind once and for all how to love, and it is tenderly, carefully, gently like a mother, and like the risen Lord who loves like a perfect mother. His feminine, nurturing side appears often in the New Testament in his attitudes, words, and behavior, as when we see him brooding over Jerusalem like a mother hen over her chicks (Matthew 23:37). This serious love, the steady, reliable, wise love of one who wants all beings to thrive joyfully in life, is almost palpable in Jesus' words to Peter today. All aspects of his maternal caring coalesce in the magnificent passage you read today, where his mature love for Peter transforms Peter's immature love for him into genuine love. Under Jesus' influence, Peter, an unreliable man without a purpose, becomes a spiritual leader for all time.

Christ transmitted his great teaching about sacred love through the tranquil image of a shepherd quietly tending a flock of sheep and lambs. A shepherd, like a mother, is entrusted with caring for others, a sacred work that continues in the evening when most work has come to an end. Christ carefully chose this simple, bucolic image to teach us to care for one another, to pay attention to one another peacefully:

- *At the depths of our being where the soul is flooded with grace, we all long to love in the way Christ loved: unconditionally. Are you aware of this longing in yourself?*
- *How can you deepen your practice of unconditional love?*
- *Can you be more supportive of another's journey? Less controlling? More sensitive? As willing to listen as to talk?*

MEDITATION: LOVING UNCONDITIONALLY

Christ's teaching about sacred love is the pathway to the most joyful and rewarding life possible. Allow his magnificent words to sink deeply into your soul, to inspire you and help you practice the sacred art of self-giving love. When we serve as an instrument of compassion in other people's lives, when we relieve their suffering or improve the quality of their lives, we feel relief from our own concerns as well as peace. Pain that we have experienced in our own lives becomes useful and purposeful. Life takes on fresh meaning. The more we choose to help those in need, the more joyful we feel; the more rewarded; the more whole and fulfilled. Think of one small action of self-giving love that you can carry out today. It may be as simple as holding back so that another person can be affirmed; or giving a friend the gift of faith by sharing with them some of the luminous words that you are about to read; or the spiritual beauty that you are about to experience reading them. Here, to help you decide how to give away your love today, are some of the most beautiful words in Western literature:

I was hungry, and you gave me food,
I was thirsty, and you gave me drink,
I was a stranger, and you welcomed me,
I was naked, and you clothed me,
I was sick, and you visited me,
I was in prison and you came to me. . . .

"Lord, when did we see you hungry and feed you,
or thirsty and give you drink?
And when did we see you a stranger and welcome you,
or naked and clothe you?
And when did we see you sick or in prison and visit you?" . . .

". . . as you did it to one of the least of these my brothers,
you did it to me."

MATTHEW 25:35–40

Practice 5

———◆———

JOURNAL REFLECTION: NURTURING OTHERS

In the Tenth Way of Light, Jesus tells his followers to relate to one another and to others as he has related to them, from an open heart willing to give: "Feed my sheep," he tells Peter, "tend my lambs," and we are asked to do the same. In your journal today, write your answer to one or more of the following questions:

• *What precisely does it mean to you to "feed" and "look after" Christ's flock? List ten ways in which we could all engage in "feeding" and "looking after" others today.*

• *Would you like to be more nurturing and caring? If so, list three areas of your life where you can open your heart to that.*

• *How can you practice Christlike nurturing when you are away from home, say, at the office, at school, traveling, or online? In what other situations?*

Practice 6

———◆———

INSIGHTS AND ILLUMINATIONS

Each moment from all sides rushes to us
The summons to love.
Do you want to come with us?
This is not the time to stay at home
But to go out and give yourself to the garden.

RUMI

There is no such thing as "my" bread. All bread is ours and is given to me, to others through me, and to me through others. For not only bread but all things necessary for sustenance in this life are given on loan to us with others, and because of others, and to others through us.

MEISTER ECKHART

To watch over a man who grieves is a more urgent duty than to think of God.

ELIE WIESEL

Being in touch with the kind of suffering we encountered during the war can heal us of some of the suffering we experience when our lives are not meaningful or useful.

THICH NHAT HANH

As surely as God is our Father is he our Mother.

JULIAN OF NORWICH

I suddenly saw the secret beauty of their hearts . . . the person that each one is in God's eyes. If only they could see themselves as they really are . . . there would be no more war, no more hatred, no more cruelty, no more greed. I suppose the big problem would be that we would all fall down and worship each other.

THOMAS MERTON

I live in the Sea always and know the Road.

EMILY DICKINSON

Practice 7

◆

RELEASING YOUR CREATIVITY: DRAWING A MANDALA

You will need a sheet of paper about eight and a half by eleven inches (or any size you prefer) and colored pencils, pens, markers, crayons, or other drawing materials. Draw a large circle or square, then, with the Tenth Station of Light in your heart, begin filling in the contents. Be as simple or as intricate as you like; include people, animals, growing things, geometric patterns—anything that comes up—without coercion or censorship from the inner critic.

When you have finished, ponder your mandala. Look at the different elements in it. Most likely, it is trying to teach you something. What is the teaching? How does it relate to the Tenth Station of Light? Does it contain guidance for your journey today? What is the center like? Does it suggest the divine center of life?

Practice 8

PRAYER FOR TODAY: THE TWENTY-THIRD PSALM

The Lord is my shepherd.
I shall not want.
He makes me to lie down in green pastures.
He restores my soul
He guides me
in paths of saving justice
for his name's sake.

Even though I walk through the valley of the shadow of death
I fear no evil;
for you are with me;
your staff is there
to comfort me.

You prepare a table before me
in the presence of my enemies;

you anoint my head with oil,
my cup overflows.
Surely goodness and kindness will follow me
all the days of my life;
and I will dwell in the house of the Lord
forever.

PSALM 23:1–6

Practice 9

ASKING FOR A SPIRITUAL GIFT

What spiritual gift or blessing would you like to receive today?

Ask, and it will be given to you;
search, and you will find;
knock, and the door will be opened to you.
For the one who asks always receives;
the one who searches always finds;
the one who knocks will always have the door opened to him.

MATTHEW 7:7–8

Practice 10

GIVING BACK
TO THE COMMUNITY

Think of a simple way to "give back" to life today as an expression of gratitude for all the blessings you receive.

JESUS SENDS THE DISCIPLES INTO THE WORLD

And he said to them, "Go into all the world, and
preach the gospel to the whole creation."
MARK 16:15

Practice 1

RELAXATION AND CENTERING: TRAINING YOURSELF FOR HAPPINESS

Begin your practice today by sitting in a comfortable, upright position, hands resting in your lap, eyes closed, feet flat on the floor. Allow your spine to be as straight as possible without tightening any muscles.

Become aware of your breathing, gently watching the ebb and flow of the breaths to begin shutting out distractions and to center. Now bring to mind an experience of happiness. Picture in detail where you were, who was with you, and what it was that elicited the happy feelings. Remember as vividly as you can if you were smiling, laughing, talking, or listening. Recall how wonderful it was to be in that warm and healthy, positive, open state, free of ego concerns, fully alive. Allow yourself to feel the happiness as completely as you can.

After a minute or so, begin to let go of the mental picture of the experience without losing awareness of the feeling-state. As you allow the memory to slip away, continue to feel happy. Rest peacefully in this wholesome feeling-state for a few more minutes. This is a healthy energy to bring to your practice of the Way of Light and to your daily activities.

Practice 2

♦

READING THE ELEVENTH STORY

Meanwhile the eleven disciples set out for Galilee, to the mountain where Jesus had directed them. And when they saw him, they fell down before him, though some hesitated. Jesus came up and spoke to them. He said, "All authority in heaven and on earth has been given to me. Go therefore, make disciples of all the nations, baptize them in the name of the Father and of the Son and of the Holy Spirit, and teach them to observe all the commands I gave you. And know that I am with you always; yes, to the end of time."

MATTHEW 28:16–20

Practice 3

◆

IMAGINING YOURSELF IN THE STORY

To pray with your whole self—body, soul, and mind—allow your senses to come to life through the following practice, entering personally into the sacred event as though it were taking place right now and you were there.

Imagine that you are one of the original disciples and have walked with the others to a favorite mountain where you have gathered with Jesus in the past on many wonderful occasions. He told you to meet him here today and clearly has an important teaching in mind. What are you feeling and thinking as you wait for him to arrive?

Now he appears, and you all sit down at a favorite place. What is it like? What flowers and plants are growing on this mountain? What other living things do you see or hear or smell? What kind of view do you see in the distance?

Jesus has assembled you here to give you what history will name "the Great Commission," and it pertains to the heart of your work after the Ascension. He is going to ask a great deal of you, and it is not only a request, it is an instruction. He is going to tell you what he wants you to do. How do you feel about that?

Now he explains that he wants you to leave your beloved Galilee and travel all over the known world to teach what he has been teaching you all these years, and to baptize people in the name of God, the Christ, and the Spirit of Christ. Look around at the disciples. Do they grasp the awesome responsibility that he is giving them? How are they responding? You have the advantage of hindsight. You know that the apostles will indeed go into the world and do exactly what Jesus tells them to do, but what is their first reaction? Go over to Peter and ask him how he feels about this commission. What does Peter say to you? How do you reply?

Practice 4
—————◆—————

MEDITATION:
SACRED AUTHORITY

Read the following words very slowly, pausing as often as you wish to reflect.

When Jesus speaks, there is always love and a firm tone of authority in his voice, the tone of one who knows exactly who he is and what he is meant to do. It is a voice born of self-confidence, proven dependability, learning, and expertise, and a God-given right to influence others. As in the Tenth Station also, Jesus addresses the disciples directly and umambiguously with frank, fatherly energy. He does not ask them, invite them, suggest, request, counsel, or guide them to leave everything behind and go into foreign countries, not knowing what lies ahead. He delivers a direct instruction that is more like a commandment than a teaching, and it leaves no room to say no. "Go and teach all nations."

And then comes the message of love: "And remember, I am with you always." Like a father whose sons are leaving home to go off and earn their living, he sends them away with unconditional love, reminding them that he will always be with them in their hearts, in mind, in spirit, protecting and strengthening them.

We today are in the position of the disciples. We have inherited the love, the authoritative message, and a considerable measure of inner authority to use well. There is a beautiful message of faith and love to be spread across the world, and those who receive it as an inheritance are called to pass it on confidently.

The artist Gauguin wrote three perennial questions on a painting of paradisal Tahiti: "Who are we? Where did we come from? Where are we going?" We people of Resurrection-faith have the answers to those questions. We know who we are, where we came from, and where we are going, because we know who is calling us. These convictions are the source of our own sacred authority, of our right and duty to influence others, as parents, teachers, moral beings, artists of our own lives, and citizens in unjust societies. Let us use our authority well. It is a spark of the divine in the soul, and the brightness of the world is a direct result of the brightness of our souls.

- *Are you aware of your own sacred authority?*
- *Where and when do you try to influence others? Are you able to speak with the courage of your convictions without being controlling?*
- *Speaking authoritatively entails confidence in God and self-confidence as well as trust in one's conscience. Do you see these three factors in yourself?*
- *If you are a parent, are you raising your children with a balance of love and authority?*

Practice 5

———◆———

JOURNAL REFLECTION: WHERE ARE YOU GOING?

To speak with authority is to speak directly. The word "direct" comes from the Latin word *dirigere,* which means "to put straight," and Christ's firm and loving words in the Scriptures "put us straight" in the sense of helping us decide which door to open, which road to take, whether or not we are going in the right direction, of if we are stuck, lost, or have veered off the path. In your journal today write a response to the question: "Where are you going?" Answer in terms of your spiritual journey.

Practice 6

INSIGHTS AND ILLUMINATIONS

If you can, spread the teachings of the Sacred Path and
Lead the way of compassion.
Help lost souls to cultivate the light.

TAOIST WISDOM (TRANSLATED BY EVA WONG)

O, God
be with me,
for the ocean is so wide,
and my boat is so small.

PRAYER OF A
BRETON FISHERMAN

The spirit of the Lord Yahweh has been given to me,
for Yahweh has anointed me.
He has sent me to bring good news to the poor,
to bind up hearts that are broken;
to proclaim liberty to captives,
freedom to those in prison; . . .
To comfort those who mourn . . .
And to give them a garland in exchange for ashes.

ISAIAH 61:1, 2C, 3B

Lord, in the presence of Your love, I ask that you unite my work with Your
great work, and bring it to fulfillment. As a drop of water poured into a
river becomes one with the flowing waters, so may all I do become part of
all that you do. So that those with whom I live and work may also be drawn
to your love.

GERTRUDE OF HELFTA

Be doers of the word, and not hearers only.

JAMES 1:22

And now, may kindly Columba guide you
to be an isle in the sea,
a hill on the shore,
a star in the night,
a staff for the weak.

CELTIC ORAL TRADITION

Practice 7

◆

RELEASING YOUR CREATIVITY: FINDING A SIMPLE WAY TO SERVE

Which local, national, or international cause do you find so pressing that you want to do something about it? Say child hunger; treatment of immigrants; the plight of refugees; violence; war; explicit sexuality in the media; universal health care; elder neglect; or another cause. Challenge your creativity today to find something you can do, no matter how small and seemingly insignificant.

If action isn't appropriate for you right now or if you are too pressed for time, consider selecting your preferred cause and finding a creative way to respond to it, say through prayer, perhaps in an online prayer group. Or you might consider a silent, wordless prayer of intention by offering a minute or more of silence for the specific intention as often as you can.

What other approach could you take?

Practice 8

———◆———

PRAYER FOR TODAY:
"GIVE ME SOMEONE"

Lord,
when I am famished,
  give me someone who needs food;
when I am thirsty,
  give me someone who needs water;
when I am cold,
  send me someone to warm;
when I am hurting,
  send me someone to console;
when my cross becomes heavy,
  give me another's cross to share;
when I am poor,
  lead someone needy to me;
when I have no time,
  give me someone to help for a moment;
when I am humiliated,
  give me someone to praise;
when I am discouraged,
  give me someone to encourage;
when I need another's understanding,
  give me someone who needs mine;
when I need someone to take care of me,
  send me someone to care for;
when I think of myself,
  turn my thoughts toward another.

SOURCE UNKNOWN
(TRANSLATED BY MARY MCCARTHY)

Practice 9
———◆———
ASKING FOR A SPIRITUAL GIFT

What spiritual gift or blessing would you like to receive today?

Ask, and it will be given to you;
search, and you will find;
knock, and the door will be opened to you.
For the one who asks always receives;
the one who searches always finds;
the one who knocks will always have the door opened to him.

MATTHEW 7:7–8

Practice 10
———◆———
GIVING BACK
TO THE COMMUNITY

Think of a simple way to "give back" to life today as an expression of gratitude for all the blessings you receive.

THE RISEN CHRIST ASCENDS INTO HEAVEN

He was lifted up while they looked on.

ACTS 1:9

Practice 1

RELAXATION AND CENTERING: COORDINATING THE MANTRA WITH THE OUT-BREATH

Begin your practice today by sitting in a comfortable, upright position, hands resting in your lap, eyes closed, feet flat on the floor. Allow your spine to be as straight as possible without tightening any muscles.

You are going to coordinate your mantra, your sacred word or phrase, with the breathing practice today. (For more on the mantra, see pp. 79–80.) Breathe naturally, allowing the breaths to come and go easily and gently. Let each exhalation flow naturally and softly after each inhalation, like the turning of the tides. Let the breaths follow the gentle rhythm of your respiration without any effort to control. After a minute or so, begin to coordinate your mantra with the exhalation, saying it silently and very slowly as you breathe out, pausing before taking the next in-breath. Make the pause as short or as long as you wish, so long as you remain comfortable throughout the practice. Continue praying the mantra once with each out-breath. Repeat for a minute or two, resting in the joyful comfort of this exercise.

Practice 2

READING THE TWELFTH STORY

As he said this, he was lifted up while they looked on, and a cloud took him from their sight. They were still staring into the sky when suddenly two men in white were standing near them, and they said, "Why are you men from Galilee standing here looking into the sky? Jesus, who has been taken up from you into heaven, this same Jesus will come back in the same way as you have seen him go there."

ACTS 1:9–11

Practice 3

IMAGINING YOURSELF IN THE STORY

To pray with your whole self—body, soul, and mind—allow your senses to come to life through the following practice, entering personally into the sacred event as though it were taking place right now and you were there.

Imagine today that you have accompanied Jesus and his followers on the half-mile walk from Jerusalem to the Mount of Olives that you have taken with him often. What do you feel as you anticipate the story or parable or other teaching that he has in mind for today? Do you have any reason to suspect that this might be the last time you will ever be with him like this?

Jesus leads you to a favorite spot on the mountainside by an especially beautiful grove of shimmering olive trees. While you wait for him to sit down, you look around at the countryside extending below and the breathtaking view in the distance. What do you see? What do you hear? Bend down and touch the earth. How does it feel? What will you most remember in the future about the natural loveliness in this scene?

You turn your gaze back toward Jesus, and he is no longer there. He has disappeared as suddenly as he appeared on that glorious Easter Sunday some six weeks ago. What is that like for you? Before there is time to think clearly, two angels in radiant white clothing are at your side, explaining, comforting, reminding you how Jesus has been preparing you for this day. Jesus told his disciples that he would complete his historical life on earth by ascending into heaven, and today is the day. What is the impact on you of the angel's message?

Jesus also taught that he will come back one day. Look around at the disciples. Does the promise of his return seem to soften the pain of their separation from Jesus? Go over to Peter to share with him what you are feeling and thinking. How does he respond to you?

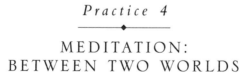

Practice 4

MEDITATION:
BETWEEN TWO WORLDS

Read the following words very slowly, pausing as often as you wish to reflect.

Luke relates in his Gospel that before Jesus leaves his beloved friends on the Mount of Olives, he lifts his hands and blesses them. Instead of saying that he embraces them one last time or delivers one last unforgettable teaching, he says good-bye through an ancient ritual gesture that is more powerful and meaningful than words. Because the blessing is a sign of the coming together of heaven and earth, of the invisible and the visible, it serves as a priestly reminder to the people on Mount Olivet, and to ourselves, of our closeness to the God we know in our hearts. This poignant final act of love says one last time that the veil between the Holy Spirit and the human spirit is very thin, and God is always with us.

The message is reinforced by the setting of the Ascension on a mountain, the archetypal place in nature where earth and heaven meet. Here on this sacred ground the earth's lush, sensual beauty mirrors the invisible realm of pure love more vividly than anywhere else. There is a feeling of transcendence on a mountain, and a view of a golden desert in the distance can suddenly turn into a mystical vision of God. It is a reminder that our lives and our plans will always intersect with God's amazing surprises.

Christ's blessing is a symbolic prayer for his friends, including ourselves, to remember that when he physically leaves the earth, his mystical presence will remain forever to protect and encourage them with endless, unpredictable blessings. In the Beatitudes he said, "Blessed are you . . ." which many languages translate as "Happy are you . . ." So it is not unreasonable to say that Christ's last blessing of his disciples is a wish for their happiness, and ours.

• *Have you prayed on a mountaintop, by the ocean, or in other settings of natural beauty?*

• *How might it deepen your spiritual life if you did some of the Way of Light practices outdoors in the summer in a beautiful place?*

• *You are approaching the end of the Way of Light. How has it affected your spirituality up to now? Have you become a little more open and awake? More self-reflective? More sensitive to others' needs?*

Practice 5

———◆———

JOURNAL REFLECTION:
SPIRITUAL UNDERSTANDING

It would seem that Christ's leaving his friends alone on Mount Olivet must have been a time of enormous sadness and grief. They lost his physical presence once at his execution, then he reappeared, and now they lose him for a second time, this time permanently. Yet the Gospels do not at all present the parting as an occasion of sorrow, but rather as a joyful time that is part of the working out of God's plan for humankind. Luke writes, "They returned to Jerusalem with great joy, and they were continually in the temple blessing God" (Luke 24:52–53).

How can you similarly change an experience of loss into a welcoming ground for spiritual understanding? Write about a specific example in your journal today.

Practice 6

———◆———

INSIGHTS AND ILLUMINATIONS

Work of the eyes is done, now
go and do heart-work.
RAINER MARIA RILKE

I am the wind that breathes upon the sea,
I am the wave on the ocean,
I am the murmur of leaves rustling,
I am the rays of the sun,
I am the beam of the moon and stars,

I am the power of trees growing,
I am the bud breaking into blossom,
I am the movement of the salmon swimming,
I am the courage of the wild boar fighting,
I am the speed of the stag running,
I am the strength of the ox pulling the plough,
I am the thoughts of all people
Who praise my beauty and grace.

ANCIENT WELSH WISDOM

I am fully assured
that neither death nor life,
nor angels nor principalities,
nor things present nor things to come,
nor powers, nor height nor depth,
nor anything else in all creation,
shall separate us from the love of God
in Christ Jesus our Lord.

ROMANS 8:38–39

Now Jesus did many other signs in the presence of the disciples which are
not written in this book; but these are written that you may believe that
Jesus is the Christ, the Son of God, and that believing you may have life in
his name.

JOHN 20:30–31

The eye in which I see God is the eye in which God sees me. My eye and
God's eye are one seeing and one knowing and one loving.

MEISTER ECKHART

Practice 7

RELEASING YOUR CREATIVITY: DIALOGUING WITH A PRAYER

Read the prayer that follows in Practice 8, "You Are Christ's Hands." Then slowly and contemplatively say the first line of the prayer. Then add your own line as though you were dialoguing with Saint Teresa. Next say her second line, then add one of your own. Continue like this through the entire prayer, stopping after each line of Teresa's to create a line of your own. As her prayer has seven lines, yours will contain fourteen. When you have finished, ask yourself if the prayer came more alive for you. Is it more meaningful now? What else happened as you did this practice?

Practice 8

PRAYER FOR TODAY: "YOU ARE CHRIST'S HANDS"

Christ has no body now on earth but yours,
  no hands but yours,
  no feet but yours,
Yours are the eyes through which
  Christ looks with compassion at the world;
Yours are the feet with which he is to go about doing good;
Yours are the hands with which he blesses people now.

TERESA OF ÁVILA

Practice 9

———◆———

ASKING FOR A SPIRITUAL GIFT

What spiritual gift or blessing would you like to receive today?

Ask, and it will be given to you;
search, and you will find;
knock, and the door will be opened to you.
For the one who asks always receives;
the one who searches always finds;
the one who knocks will always have the door opened to him.

MATTHEW 7:7–8

Practice 10

———◆———

GIVING BACK
TO THE COMMUNITY

Think of a simple way to "give back" to life today as an expression of gratitude for all the blessings you receive.

WAITING WITH MARY IN THE UPPER ROOM

All these joined in continuous prayer.

ACTS 1:14

Practice 1

RELAXATION AND CENTERING: REPEATING THE NAME OF MARY

Begin your practice today by sitting in a comfortable, upright position, hands resting in your lap, eyes closed, feet flat on the floor. Allow your spine to be as straight as possible without tightening any muscles.

If you are at home, place on your home altar an image or symbol of Mary of Nazareth, the mother of Jesus. If you are praying the Way of Light in a church, sit by a statue of Mary or an altar to her. Keep your eyes focused as much as you can on the image or symbol that you have chosen. Begin by taking three slow, deep breaths. Allow yourself with each breath to sink deeper into the sacred center of your soul. When you are ready, quietly and reverently say the word "Mary." This is your mantra (sacred word or phrase) today. Repeat the name very slowly for a few minutes. If you wish, coordinate repetitions with the out-breath, slowly repeating Mary's name each time you exhale.

Practice 2

—— ◆ ——

READING THE THIRTEENTH STORY

So from the Mount of Olives, as it is called, they went back to Jerusalem, a short distance away, no more than a sabbath walk; and when they reached the city they went to the Upper Room where they were staying; there were Peter and John and James and Andrew, Philip and Thomas, Bartholomew and Matthew, James the son of Alphaeus and Simon the Zealot, and Jude the brother of James. All these joined in continuous prayer, together with several women, including Mary the mother of Jesus, and with his brothers.

ACTS I:12–14

Practice 3

—— ◆ ——

IMAGINING YOURSELF IN THE STORY

To pray with your whole self—body, soul, and mind—allow your senses to come to life through the following practice, entering personally into the sacred event as though it were taking place right now and you were there.

Imagine yourself once again in the company of the disciples in the Upper Room, where you have all gathered around Mary, the beloved and revered mother of Jesus, who is deep in prayer. All of the apostles and disciples, male and female, are there, including of course the well-to-do owner, who always provided this safe haven for Jesus and his friends. Look around this cherished room where you have been present for so many sacred occasions. What details do you observe today? Whom do you recognize? Mary Magdalene? Peter? Joanna? James?

Notice how everyone is seated around Mary, leaning toward her. What other signs do you see of the way they feel about her? What is it like to be with her and, especially, to pray with her? How would you describe her appearance? Swarthy, earthy, and grounded like many Middle Eastern women? Is her veil like those worn by Middle Eastern women today? How does she differ in this active situation of prayer from the old cultural image of her as sweet and passive?

The whole community is praying now, fervently, ecstatically, rapturously praising and thanking God. Excitement in the room crescendoes, as though something wonderful were about to happen. Have you ever prayed like this? Try it. What is it like for you?

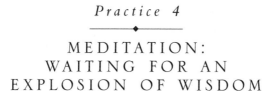

Practice 4

MEDITATION: WAITING FOR AN EXPLOSION OF WISDOM

Read the following words very slowly, pausing as often as you wish to reflect.

We meet Mary the mother of Jesus for the first time in the Way of Light in the final days of the post-Resurrection period. She is in the Upper Room with the adoring disciples gathered all around her waiting and praying fervently for the Spirit of Christ to come. She is a center of warmth and illumination for the disciples, as she is for ourselves today after two thousand years of endless veneration in glorious poetry, stained glass windows, statues, and chapels dedicated to her all over the world. In the twelfth century alone, over fifty soaring cathedrals were named for her.

Her face recalls her son's; her words and gestures are reminiscent of his. She is the only person who has ever been fully informed about Jesus, the closest to him of anyone on earth, the one who knew her child more intimately than anyone else, and the one who lost the most when he died.

Like thousands of broken mothers of murdered sons, of sons killed in war, and of *desaparecidos*, those who disappear in occupied countries, dictatorships, and ghettoes—in her time and in our own—she has undergone a soul-shattering experience. But fifty enlightening days have transpired since then, bringing appearances of the risen Christ and with him the return of trust, hope, belief in goodness and love, and healing.

Now a tried and tested woman in her late forties, rapidly matured by a richness of spiritual experience that she ponders deeply, Mary reveals the same receptivity to the divine that she exhibited in her youth at the Annunciation, when she learned she would give birth to the Christ. Just as on that providential day when she was called to the awesome responsibility of mothering a child with a world-shaking destiny, so today she meets a challenging situation by saying yes. Yes to faith, yes to love, yes to waiting as long as it takes until the Holy Spirit comes.

But Mary's journey does not stop there. She is on pilgrimage and always will be in the hearts of humankind, an exemplar of wisdom and openness and receptivity to the invitations of God. Through the *imitatio Mariae*, the imitation of Mary, who is as essential to the working out of the divine mystery as her son, we journey with her. Like Mary, we can "ponder things in the heart" (Luke 2:19, 51) and find the willingness and courage to say yes to life's invitations, "Yes, I accept. Yes, I will not run away."

• *What does it mean to you to be "on pilgrimage with Mary"?*
• *Does journeying with Mary free you of the desire to impress?*
• *Do you think of yourself as receptive to divine invitations and surprises, or do you sometimes put up resistance? Do you need to stop getting in your own way?*
• *What aspect of the* imitatio Mariae, *imitation of Mary, would you like to be open to? Her simplicity? Her acceptance? Her ability to face hardship? Or what other quality?*

Practice 5

———◆———

JOURNAL REFLECTION: WAITING WITH FAITH

One of the most treasured Christian spiritual practices is a devotion to Mary, the Rosary, and its popularity in our time is spreading like wildfire. Pray a decade of the Rosary, then respond in your journal to one or more of the following questions.

> • *Is praying the Rosary like being in the Upper Room with Mary, waiting with faith?*
> • *What might be the benefits of praying the Rosary (or a decade of it) on a regular basis, say weekdays?*
> • *Have you ever tried praying the Rosary while walking? If so, have you noticed boredom turn into contemplation?*

Practice 6

———◆———

INSIGHTS AND ILLUMINATIONS

My soul proclaims the greatness of the Lord,
and my spirit exults in God my Savior.
Because he has looked upon his lowly handmaid.
Yes, from this day forward all generations will call me blessed;
for the almighty has done great things for me.
Holy is his name,
and his mercy reaches from age to age for those who fear him.
He has shown the power of his arm,
he has routed the proud of heart.

He has pulled down princes from their thrones and exalted the lowly.
The hungry he has filled with good things,
and the rich he has sent empty away.
He has come to the help of Israel his servant, mindful of his mercy
—according to the promise he made to our ancestors—
of his mercy to Abraham and to his descendants forever.

LUKE 1:47–55

Blessed is she who believed that the promise made her by the Lord would be
fulfilled.

LUKE 1:45

We are the mother of Christ when we carry him in our heart.

SAINT FRANCIS OF ASSISI

My soul yearns for you in the night;
yes, my spirit within me keeps vigil for you.

ISAIAH 26:9

I am a feather on the breath of God.

HILDEGARD OF BINGEN

Court [wisdom] with all your soul,
and with all your might keep her ways;
go after her and seek her;
she will reveal herself to you;
once you hold her, do not let her go.
For in the end you will find rest in her
and she will take the form of joy for you.

ECCLESIASTICUS 6:26–28

Practice 7

—————◆—————

RELEASING YOUR CREATIVITY:
CREATING A "MARY PRAYER"

Create a beautiful "Mary Prayer" (a "Mary Mantra") in the tradition of the Jesus Prayer. For example, "Mary, mother of us all, be with us." "Mary, mother of the poor, have mercy." "Mary mother of the ill, be gracious." "Come, Mary, come." "Mary, give me wisdom (or comfort, strength, guidance, patience, and so on)."

Recite your Mary Prayer slowly like a mantra when you find you need to still your mind or renew spiritual energy. It will calm you in overly emotional times, and it will bring new energy into your heart when you feel empty or depressed. If you fall asleep at night saying the prayer, you may find it repeating itself in your heart when you awaken.

Practice 8

—————◆—————

PRAYER FOR TODAY: "HAIL MARY"

Hail Mary
full of grace,
the Lord
is with you.
Blessed
are you
among women
and blessed
is the fruit
of your womb,

Jesus.
Holy Mary
Mother of God
pray for us
now
and at the hour of our death.
    Amen

Practice 9

ASKING FOR A SPIRITUAL GIFT

What spiritual gift or blessing would you like to receive today?

Ask, and it will be given to you;
search, and you will find;
knock, and the door will be opened to you.
For the one who asks always receives;
the one who searches always finds;
the one who knocks will always have the door opened to him.

MATTHEW 7:7–8

Practice 10

GIVING BACK TO THE COMMUNITY

Think of a simple way to "give back" to life today as an expression of gratitude for all the blessings you receive.

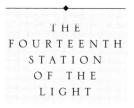

J E S U S   S E N D S
T H E   H O L Y   S P I R I T

Something appeared to them that seemed like tongues of fire;
and they were all filled with the Holy Spirit.

ACTS 2:3–4

Practice 1

R E L A X A T I O N   A N D   C E N T E R I N G :
V I S U A L I Z I N G   G O L D E N   L I G H T

Begin your practice today by sitting in a comfortable, upright position, hands resting in your lap, eyes closed, feet flat on the floor. Allow your spine to be as straight as possible without tightening any muscles.

Take three deep breaths to begin focusing your attention and allowing any tension to dissipate. Now imagine golden light above your head, shining down on you. Imagine this beautiful light very slowly descending within you and all around you, filling every cell with spiritual power, love, and peace. Imagine your head filling with golden light; then your neck; then your shoulders. Little by little allow the light to descend into your arms; hands;

chest. Then into your abdominal region and, very slowly, the rest of your torso. Be aware of the sacred energies filling your whole body. Imagine the light descending into your legs; your feet; to the tips of your toes. Savor for a moment the fullness of energy, love, and peace that floods your entire being.

Practice 2

◆

READING THE FOURTEENTH STORY

When Pentecost day came around, they had all met in one room, when suddenly they heard what sounded like a powerful wind from heaven, the noise of which filled the entire house in which they were sitting; and something appeared to them that seemed like tongues of fire; these separated and came to rest on the head of each of them. They were all filled with the Holy Spirit and began to speak in tongues as the Spirit gave them the gift of speech.

ACTS 2:1−4

Practice 3

◆

IMAGINING YOURSELF
IN THE STORY

To pray with your whole self—body, soul, and mind—allow your senses to come to life through the following practice, entering personally into the sacred event as though it were taking place right now and you were there.

Today you have reached the magnificent culmination of the Way of Light. See yourself in your imagination seated with the disciples in a joyful circle around Mary, praying fervently for the Spirit of Christ to come to you. Notice how transported everyone appears through the mystical beauty of praying with her. Can you feel the sacred passion in the room rising toward a crescendo? Is the feeling like ecstasy?

Suddenly you hear a sound like a roaring wind and the room fills with blazing light and heat. You look at Mary and see a flame burning over her head. You look at Peter and see a flame pouring down on him, too. So with James and John and Mary Magdalene and everyone in the room, including you, what is it like to be with these great souls in this holy place at this awesome moment?

As the flames burn, the praying grows and intensifies until it reaches a mystical peak, and all at once, all together, you hear strange, mysterious, glorious sounds. Have you ever been with people praying in tongues? Notice what a holy and beautiful experience it is, how all the voices blend in perfect harmony like a choir of angels praising God.

Are you aware of what a precious gift you have been given? A gift you will take out into the world with you to serve God's purposes for the rest of your life? You have taken part in marvels, and your life will never be the same again. Wait until the room becomes quiet, then turn to the disciple beside you and share what you are thinking and feeling. How does this person reply to you?

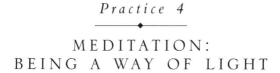

Practice 4

MEDITATION:
BEING A WAY OF LIGHT

Read the following words very slowly, pausing as often as you wish to reflect.

With this amazing outpouring of fire into the disciples' bodies and souls on Pentecost, the Way of Light comes to a close that is also a new beginning. Christ sends a burning spirit to inflame his followers with faith and love and passionate commitment to teach and heal in the same way he taught and healed them. The ecstatic experience puts an end to the doubts and anxieties that plagued Jesus' followers when he died, reassuring them about the huge purpose in his life and death. They have been rescued from any possible ignorance of God, any possible ignorance of the mystical capacity of humankind to experience the divine. All along the Way of Light, the risen Lord graces his followers with sign after sign to help them know who he is and believe what he says, but here is a mystical experience so intense, so rapturously beautiful, so immensely compelling to those who underwent it and to those of us who hear about it, that "the way, the truth, and the life" become crystal clear: Christ is the Way, the Truth, and the Life.

Pentecost brings an explosion of wisdom, a gift of deep understanding, to humankind. As the Holy Spirit descends, the human spirit soars, penetrating into spiritual and mystical dimensions of life that the ego cannot enter. Pentecost knits Jesus' followers into a spiritual community that will seed the world with the colorful, bright beauty of faith and love. This breathtaking awakening drives Jesus' disciples into the wider world to share the astounding story of a young man who has shaken the foundations of society and moved the heart to new levels of love.

And now with this enormous infusion of wisdom in the form of a fiery vision, the Spirit of Christ inspires us to remain awake, to refuse to go back to sleep, to live with spiritual vision in the midst of busy, stressful existence day by day. The Christian Way of Light has guided us through fourteen unforgettably beautiful stories to a new awareness of living in Christ's light. We have been given a faith that is joyful, a love that is pure and unconditional, hope for tomorrow, and a way to recognize Christ in everyone we meet. Let us rejoice and be happy.

- *You have been offered tremendous grace and blessings practicing the fourteen stations of the Way of Light. What do you treasure most about your experience on this pilgrimage?*
- *Are you aware that you have all you need to be a "way of light," a person who brightens daily life for others?*
- *Are you allowing people to see that Light in you?*
- *Are you working at seeing the Light that shines in other people?*

• *Pentecost brings God down out of the obscurity of the skies once and for all into the bodies, hearts, and minds of humankind. How does the God you know in your heart differ from the God who was thought to live up in the sky?*

Practice 5

JOURNAL REFLECTION: YOUR DREAMS AND VISIONS FOR THE FUTURE

You are a member of the spiritual community that came together on Pentecost two thousand years ago and is celebrated in the last Station of Light. Journal today about your dreams and visions for the future as a member of the Family of God. Think about the repository of wisdom that you have inherited, the beauty of the Scriptures, the unique sacramental life that enables you to take part in mystery and divinity.

Practice 6

INSIGHTS AND ILLUMINATIONS

Sit with me, let a smile form on your lips, let your sun shine.
THICH NHAT HANH

When the mystery of love is unveiled to you
You exist no longer, but vanish into love.
Place before the Sun a burning candle,

You will see its brilliance disappear before that blaze,
The candle is no longer, it is Light.
There are no more signs of it;
It has become a sign.

RUMI

Make of yourself a light.

THE BUDDHA'S LAST WORDS

You are the light of the world. A city built on a hilltop cannot be hidden.

MATTHEW 5:14

And it shall come to pass afterward
that I will pour out my spirit on all flesh;
your sons and your daughters shall prophesy,
your old men shall dream dreams,
and your young men shall see visions.
And on my menservants and maidservants
in those days
I will pour out my Spirit; and they shall prophesy.

JOEL 2:28C–29; ACTS 2:18C

History rushes forward, and God is always there.

SAINT HILARY OF POITIERS

As candles burn with visible fire
to dispel the darkness of night,
so may our open hearts
illumine the world.

TRADITIONAL

Be ablaze with enthusiasm.
Let us be an alive,
burning offering
before the altar of God!

HILDEGARD OF BINGEN

May every creature abound in well-being and peace.
May every living being, weak or strong, the long and the small,
the short and the medium-sized, the poor and the great—
may every living being, seen or unseen, those dwelling far off,
those nearby, those already born, those waiting to be born—
may all attain inward peace.

TRADITIONAL BUDDHIST PRAYER

I am certain that the One who began this good work in you will bring it to
completion when the day of Christ Jesus comes.

PHILIPPIANS 1:6

Practice 7

RELEASING YOUR CREATIVITY: WRITING A PSALM OF PRAISE

Write a brief psalm of praise for the blessings you have received from practicing the Via Lucis.

Practice 8

PRAYER FOR TODAY: "GO FORWARD SECURELY"

What you hold, may you always hold. What you do, may you always do,
and never abandon. But with swift pace, light step, and unswerving feet, go
forward securely, joyfully, and lightly, on wisdom's path. Believing nothing,
agreeing with nothing, which would dissuade you from your resolution. Or

which would place a stumbling block for you on the way. So that you may offer your promises to the Most High God, in the pursuit of the sacred goals to which the Spirit has summoned you.

CLARE OF ASSISI

Practice 9

◆

ASKING FOR A SPIRITUAL GIFT

What spiritual gift or blessing would you like to receive today?

> *Ask, and it will be given to you;*
> *search, and you will find;*
> *knock, and the door will be opened to you.*
> *For the one who asks always receives;*
> *the one who searches always finds;*
> *the one who knocks will always have the door opened to him.*

MATTHEW 7:7–8

Practice 10

◆

GIVING BACK TO THE COMMUNITY

Think of a simple way to "give back" to life today as an expression of gratitude for all the blessings you receive.

After You Read This Book

Making a Pilgrimage to the Stations of the Light

A full set of all twenty-eight stations, the Stations of the Light and the Stations of the Cross, has been created at St. John's Center in Plymouth, Michigan. You will find the stations in a lovely "Via Garden" (named of course for the Via Crucis and Via Lucis, which is a wonderful, sacred place to make a pilgrimage. Due to its central location, St. John's can be comfortably reached by most modes of transportation from any part of the country. Be sure to include the children! Here is contact information:

St. John's Center for Youth and Family
44011 Five Mile Rd.
Plymouth, MI 48170
E-mail: info@sjcyf.org
Websites ("aod" stands for archdiocese of Detroit):
http://www.aodonline.org/StJohn/Contact+Us+8185/Contact+Us.htm
http://www.aodonline.org/StJohn/VirtuTour+11507/Virtual+Tour.htm
   (This site takes you on a virtual tour of the Via Garden.)
Tel: 734-414-1111
Fax: 734-414-1150

St John's has limited accommodations, so it would be wise to contact the center well in advance to make a reservation or ask about alternative accommodations in the vicinity.

By the time this book is published, additional sets of the *Stations of the*

Light may exist nearer to you or in another country you plan to visit. Online research is currently the best way to keep up with the rapid spread of the Way of Light abroad. In the U.S., it may be helpful to also telephone or e-mail your diocese for information.

Creating the Stations of the Light in Your Church

The Way of Light is a path of beautiful symbols that ought to be represented in every church, like the Stations of the Cross, and eventually will be. Then, when you go to church to pray the stations, the devotion will no longer conclude on the tragic note of the crucifixion but will continue through the beautiful and joyful events of Jesus' post-Easter life and conclude with the happiness of Pentecost.

But leadership is urgently needed! Here is an invaluable opportunity for you: Speak with your pastor about raising funds to create the Stations of the Light on the church walls or, if they don't fit there, in another appropriate location, say, a parish garden.

While you are mobilizing resources to have permanent Stations of the Light carved, sculpted, or painted you can make posters of the stations. Since posters are portable, they can be brought out as needed when your congregation or group wants to pray the Via Lucis. Posters need to be large enough for the congregation to see even from the back of the church and can be photographed to show as slides. Look for artists in your parish who will help. If your church has a school, urge teachers to have children make posters.

Creating the Stations in an Adoration Chapel

If you are fortunate enough to belong to a parish that has an adoration chapel, you may wish to help raise funds or find artists to create a set of Stations of the Light there. The profound silence and beauty found in adoration chapels makes them an ideal setting for the Way of Light.

Involving Children and Young People

In the spring of 2004, west of London in the village of Cookham, young people created a full set of all twenty-eight Stations of the Cross and "Stations of the Resurrection" (as the Stations of Light are called in Europe) that were on display in public places for two weeks. This is a wonderful model for American children in families, Christian schools, and religion classes.

Important Reminder: When you seek information online (or in libraries), try the keywords "Via Lucis" and "Stations of the Resurrection," as well as "The Way of Light" and "Stations of the Light."

Resources

Pilgrim Prayers: The Official Vatican Prayerbook for the Jubilee Year 2000, the Continuum Publishing Company, 1999, $15.95. Used copies cost only a few dollars. The book contains brief prayers for the Way of Light and beautiful colored illustrations by Sister Anna Maria di Domenico, which can be seen in Italy at San Giovanni Retondo, a monastery and town near the Adriatic across from Naples. See them at www.vialucis.net.

The Tablet: For a succinct article on the rediscovery of the inscription in the San Callisto Catacomb, see www.thetablet.UK.

Fr. Sabino Palumbieri, the Salesian priest and professor at the Pontifical Salesian University in Rome, whose spiritual group created the first Stations of the Light. His contact information is:

Prof. don Sabino Palumbieri
Universita Pontificia Salesiana
Piazza dell'Ateneo Salesiano, 1
00139 Roma RM

"Give Me a Firm Footing," a beautiful article by Fr. Palumbieri, may be found in many languages at: http://www.vatican.va/jubilee_2000/magazine/documents/ju_mag_01111997_p9_en.html.

A good U.S. website with illustrations of the Stations of the Light and music: St. Gabriel Church, 400 West High St, Minerva, Ohio 44657, tel: 330-868-4498, http://pages.eohio.net/stgabriel/title_frame.htm.

Blogs (weblogs): Look for blogsites in the UK and in other countries if you read the language. Italian is especially helpful.

This Mexican website, which offers prayers in Spanish for praying the Way of Light, illustrates each station with a powerful contemporary drawing, apparently pen and ink. Visit at: http://www.churchforum.org/info/Manual_de_Oraciones/Via_Lucis/Default.htm.

Index of Practices

MEDITATIONS:

PRAYERS:

RELAXATION AND CENTERING PRACTICES: